BUILD BETTER
BOXES

10 Projects to Improve Design and Technique

MATT KENNEY

**BLUE
HILLS**
PRESS

ACKNOWLEDGMENTS

I've always loved to make boxes. The first thing I ever made was a box, in fact. However, I wouldn't be where I am today if a former boss of mine didn't make the same joke every time I brought a new box into the office at *Fine Woodworking* magazine to show my coworkers what I was up to. He'd say that boxes are pointless because they have no function, then crack that boxes are only good for storing pot. It made me think, and I realized that he was simply wrong, because utility is not the same as purpose. A box might not have a specific utility, but it can still have a purpose: to be beautiful, to bring happiness into your life, and to be an expression of the creative forces running through you. After that I quadrupled down on my box making. So, I guess I should say thanks to that boss. But I'd rather say thanks to my parents for teaching me to believe in myself, especially when others did not, and for instilling a strong work ethic and self-discipline in me. I would not be where I am without their love, compassion, and support. I'm also grateful for my children, Grace and Elijah, for all the reasons a father loves his children, but also because my love for them allowed me to become more patient, compassionate, open, and empathetic, which in turn enabled me to become more creative. I owe Joe Mazurek a great deal, too, because he taught me to make furniture. Without his kindness and generosity, I'd probably be an adjunct professor teaching philosophy. Instead, I am happy and flourishing, making boxes and sharing my passion for furniture making. And a hearty thank you to Matthew Teague of Blue Hills Press. I emailed him before I drove home after being laid off from *Fine Woodworking* magazine and asked if he'd like to do a book together. He said yes without hesitation. This is the second book we've done. He's a great editor and sounding board, and has had a big hand in the success I've experienced over the last several years. Finally, to all the folks out there who have bought my books, taken classes with me, follow me on Instagram, or otherwise offered their support: Thank you! I am forever grateful that my work and contributions to the craft are appreciated.

CONTENTS

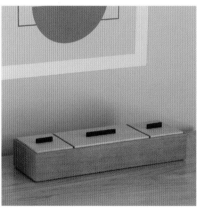

INTERLUDES:

INTRODUCTION

I've made things from wood since I was a kid. Back then it was tree forts and skateboarding ramps. My brother and I would "borrow" tools from Dad, scrounge around for plywood, lumber, and anything else we could use, then get to work. However, I did not take up serious woodworking until I was 28, when I impulsively decided to make a storage box for gardening supplies as a gift for someone. I used junky lumber and tools from a home center, and designed it myself. I had no idea what I was doing, but I loved doing it, so I kept at it. The second and third things I made were also boxes.

By the time I started working at *Fine Woodworking* magazine in 2008 (eight years after the gardening box), I had made a fair number of boxes. By the time I left the magazine, in 2018, I had not only made dozens more boxes, but also had written my first book, *52 Boxes in 52 Weeks* (Taunton Press). Although it includes a chapter about technique, and a number of other building methods are sprinkled throughout the book, it's really about my efforts to become a better designer by designing then making a bunch of boxes over the course of a year. So, I always knew that eventually I'd write a book about how I make boxes. And, well, here we are.

There are 10 boxes in this book, and I show you how to make each of them. There are measured drawings for each box, and step-by-step instructions. Read through the chapters and you'll learn how I cut miters (and spline them when the mood strikes me). Dovetails, rabbets, and finger joints are covered as well. There's some talk about milling, too, and how to create box sides that have grain flowing continuously around all for corners. Some of the boxes have drawers and look an awful lot like what most folks call furniture, so you can learn how to make and fit a drawer, and techniques for case construction. I often use veneer (both shop-made and store-bought) when making boxes, so I show you how I glue it to plywood to make lids and bottoms, and how to hide those nasty plywood edges with milk paint. Many of my boxes are lined with fabric or paper, and I cover my techniques for working with these as well. All of the boxes are finished with shellac, so there's a demonstration of how I apply it.

In short, this book is a thorough explanation of the techniques I use to make boxes, but the techniques don't make them better boxes. In fact, the book's title, *Build Better Boxes*, really isn't a reference to the boxes you'll find it. It's a call to action. I want you to get out into the shop and make better boxes, and better furniture. I hope these 10 boxes inspire you to do that and provide a solid foundation in the techniques required to make them.

If you are as inquisitive as I am, and I hope you are, then you are most likely asking yourself what makes a box better. The answer to that question has nothing to do with the techniques and tools used to make boxes and furniture. It's not about how you make the box, but why you make it. Boxes, and furniture generally, are tricky things, because they are utilitarian. In order to be a good box, it should perform its function well. That could be something as simple and nebular as "store mementos from my trips to Australia" or as narrow and clearly defined as "hold tea packets and the set of four green tea cups that my friend made."

But there is something beyond the function that matters, something bigger than utility that you should be aiming for when you make boxes and furniture: beauty, purpose, and meaning. When I design and make a box, I think about what happens to it after it leaves my shop, how it will fit into the home and the daily life

of the person who owns it. As I see it, the box's purpose is to become woven into the fabric of the owner's life, to become something valued, cherished, and loved. My goal for the box is that it become a meaningful part of their life, that it have sentimental value. Certainly, the box must perform its function well to achieve this goal, but more important, it must be beautiful. It must feel good in the hand, and beckon the owner to use it. A better box is a beautiful box, an inviting box, a meaningful box.

The techniques I demonstrate in this book are less important than what you make with them. Be thoughtful about design, pay attention to beauty, and think of the person for whom you are making the box. Embody your attention, your love, and your desire to do good in the box. Make your box better by making it an expression of your creativity, your humanity. I've tried to do that with the 10 boxes in this book, and I hope that they inspire you to get out into the shop and create work that embodies who you are and that will be cherished for generations to come.

Box 1

A SIMPLE MITERED BOX

I AM OBSESSED WITH SIMPLICITY because I believe that's where the greatest beauty and elegance are found. This is why I constantly design and make boxes that are stripped down to the core elements of a box. I figure if I can make a beautiful box from nothing more than proportions, lines, and color, then I've accomplished something wonderful and inspiring. This box is a perfect example of what's possible if you focus on just a few design elements, but refine them as much as possible. You end up with a box that's understated but graceful, that's quiet but definitely makes a strong statement, one that's heard by a large number of folks. This box is also a great, low-risk lesson in box making. You'll learn how to cut accurate miters and end up with a box that's square, and how to fit a lid and bottom that are tight but not so tight as to cause problems down the road. I'll also introduce two materials that I use over and over in my boxes: milk paint and fabric. The techniques that I use to make this box, from milling the lumber to lining the bottom with fabric, are techniques that you can use for any box. They are the foundational skills you need to make strong, square, beautiful boxes.

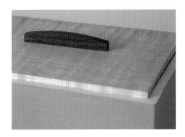

TOOLS

- Jointer
- Planer
- Bandsaw
- Tablesaw
- Dado set
- Block plane
- Rasp and file
- Rotary cutter

MATERIALS

- Basswood
- Spruce
- Walnut
- Tiger maple
- Cocobolo
- Plywood
- Fabric
- Milk Paint

PARTS LIST

PART	L	W	T
Front/Back	5"	1¾"	¼"
Ends	4"	1¾"	¼"
Lid	4⅝"	3⅝"	5/16"
Bottom	4⅝"	3⅝"	¼"
Pull	2"	5/16"	3/16"

DRAWING

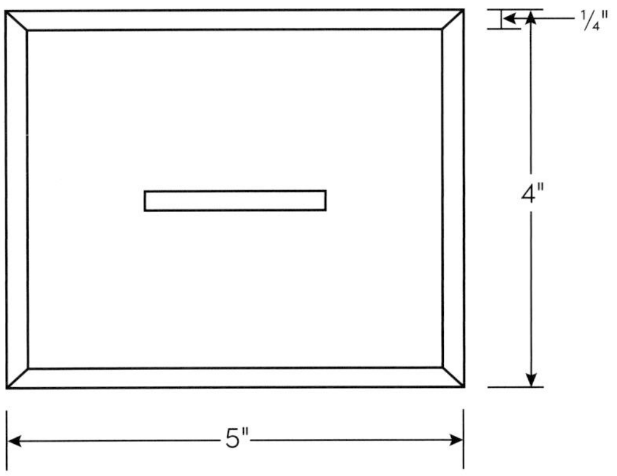

¼"
4"
5"

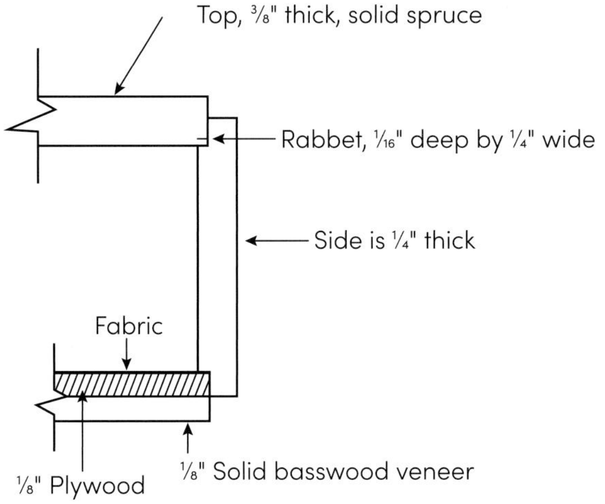

Top, ⅜" thick, solid spruce
Rabbet, 1/16" deep by ¼" wide
Side is ¼" thick
Fabric
⅛" Plywood
⅛" Solid basswood veneer

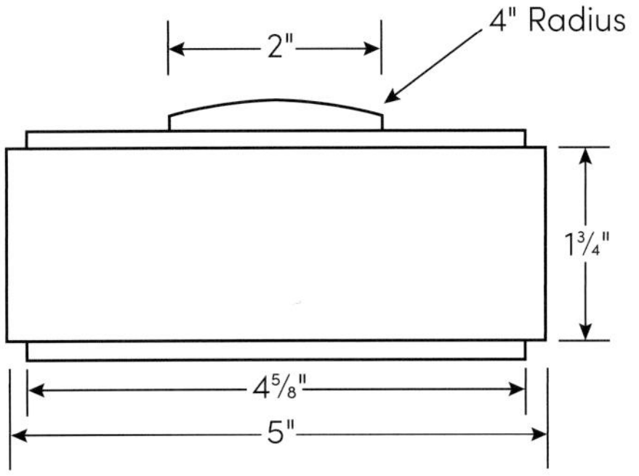

2"
4" Radius
1¾"
4⅝"
5"

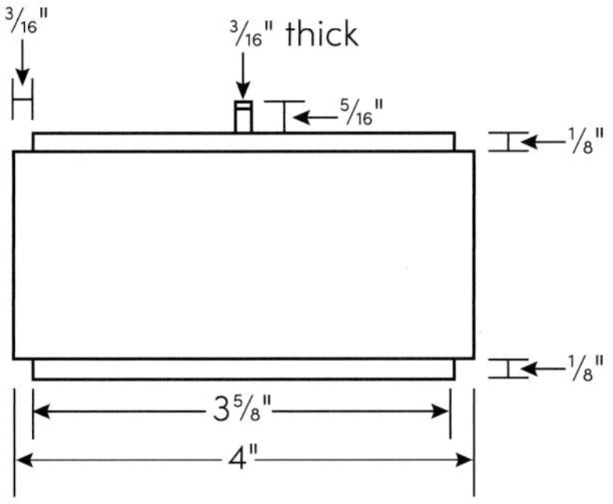

3/16"
3/16" thick
5/16"
⅛"
⅛"
3⅝"
4"

MAKE STOCK FOR THE SIDES

Because the outside of this box is painted, there's no need to worry about what the grain looks like and if it matches at all four corners. This makes it much easier to mill stock for the sides. Start with a board that's 25 – 26 in. long and ½ in. wider than the side's final width. I make this box from basswood, so that the interior is nice and bright.

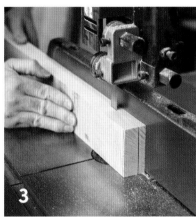

1 **JOINT THE BOARD'S FACE.** If the board is cupped, orient it concave face down. Run it over the cutterhead until the face is both flat across its width and straight along its length.

2 **SQUARE AN EDGE TO THE FACE.** The jointed face goes against the fence. Slow down the feed rate to get a cleaner, smoother edge.

3 **RESAW AT THE BANDSAW.** Cut it at least ⅜ in. thick at the bandsaw. Then run it through the planer to bring it down to ¼ in. thick.

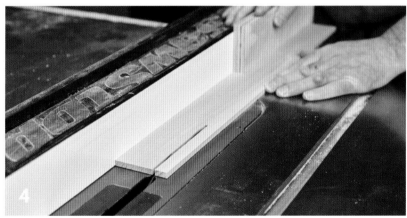

4 **RIP TO FINAL WIDTH.** Make sure the jointed edge stays tight against the rip fence, so that the opposite edge is parallel to it and straight.

5 **SAND THE INSIDE FACE.** Start with P-220 grit and work up to P-400 grit. Use a narrow sanding block. Take long strokes, which will minimize the chance of sanding a dip into the board.

CUT THE JOINERY

The rabbets around the box's top and bottom edges are identical, and cut with the same tablesaw setup. The corners are joined with miters. It's critical to cut them accurately, so take your time when setting up to cut them.

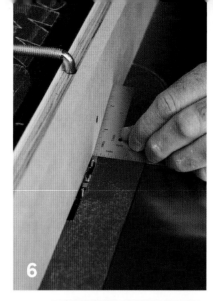

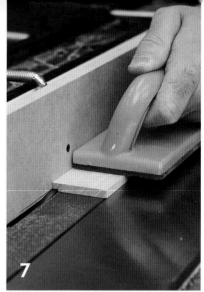

6 **SET UP FOR A RABBET.** Bury a dado set in a sacrificial fence, leaving ¼ in. exposed.

7 **CUT THE RABBET.** Use push pads to keep the board flat on the saw table and tight against the rip fence.

8 **SQUARE UP THE ENDS.** Use a crosscut sled to square one end of the board and cut away any snipe.

9 **CROSSCUT THE LONG SIDES.** Clamp a stop block to your sled's fence and cut the two 5-in.-long sides.

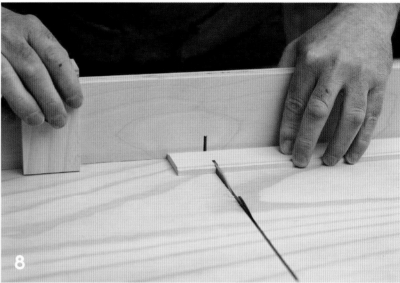

10 **SHORTEN THE STOP.** Place a 1 in. spacer block against the stop block.

11 **CUT THE SHORT SIDES.** Slide the board against the spacer and cut the two 4 in. long sides.

12 **MITER THE ENDS.** Set the tablesaw blade to 45° and position a stop block so that the blade cuts a miter without removing any length from the long side. The top edge of the side's end should align with a zero-clearance kerf cut by the blade. After cutting all the miters on the two long ends, put the 1 in. spacer block against the stop and miter the two short sides.

13 **CHECK FOR SQUARE.** For the box to glue up square, the joint must be square across its width.

14 **CONFIRM THE MITER, TOO.** If they aren't 45°, the box won't be square.

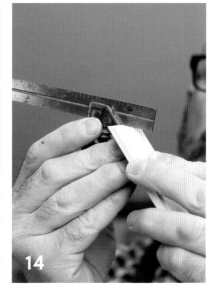

GLUE UP THE BOX

Using the right painter's tape is key: Scotch Original blue painter's masking tape doesn't slip when you close up the box, and doesn't stretch much, so it applies plenty of pressure. I prefer the 2-in.-wide version. If you can't find it, green Frog Tape works, as well.

15 **TAPE THE JOINTS.** Firmly press one side down on a piece of blue tape. Hold the mating side at an angle and press the miters together.

16 **PRESS FIRMLY.** Lay the mating side on the tape and apply pressure. Continue taping the other sides.

17 **AVOID MISTAKES.** Sides and ends of similar length are easily confused. Make sure to tape them up in this order: 5 in. side, 4 in. end, 5 in. side, 4 in. end.

18 **ADD GLUE.** Run a bead of glue down the joint. A glue bottle with a small nozzle, like the Babe Bot, makes it possible to do this neatly.

19 **SPREAD AND REAPPLY.** Cover both sides of the miters using a beveled glue stick. After a few minutes, add glue and spread again.

20 **ROLL IT UP.** Resistance as you pull the last joint closed means the stretching tape will apply more pressure. Tape the last joint in place.

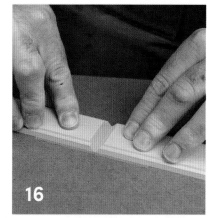

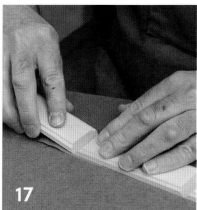

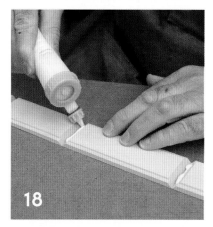

MAKE AND FIT THE BOTTOM

There are three layers to the bottom: fabric on top, plywood in the middle, and a shopsawn veneer on the bottom. With plywood at its core, the bottom is very stable and can be glued into the box.

21 **CUT A THIN VENEER.** It should be no more than ⅛ in. thick. I run the freshly bandsawn veneer through my planer and bring it down to ³⁄₃₂ in. thick, but you can also do this with a hand plane or drum sander.

22 **GLUE IT TO A PIECE OF PLYWOOD.** The plywood and veneer are the same size, about ½ in. longer and wider than the bottom's final dimensions. The glue should cover the plywood evenly, but not too thickly, because it then acts like a lubricant and the veneer might slide out of position under pressure.

23 **TAPE IN PLACE.** Adding a piece of blue painter's tape to each end reduces the chance of the veneer moving under clamping pressure.

24 **CLAMP IT UP.** A pair of ¾ in. plywood cauls spreads the pressure over the entire glue-up. Make sure that the edges of the veneers are tight against the plywood.

25 **CLEAN AN EDGE.** After removing any squeeze-out from one long side, rip the other side clean.

26 **MARK THE WIDTH.** Place the ripped side into the box just enough that it catches on a rabbet, and draw a line where the other side hits the opposite rabbet.

27 **ADJUST THE RIP FENCE.** Cut the bottom just proud of the line. Use a block plane or a sanding block to sneak up on the fit.

28 **MARK THE FINAL LENGTH.** Square one end and mark the bottom's length just as you did its width.

29 **TRIM THE LENGTH.** Cut to the line and test the fit. If it's too long, you can cut it carefully with the saw, sand it to fit, or use a block plane and shooting board to dial in the length.

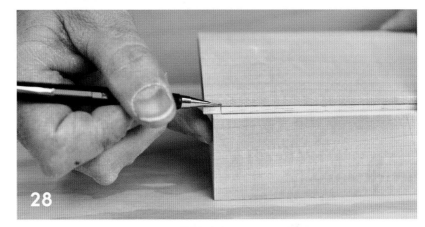

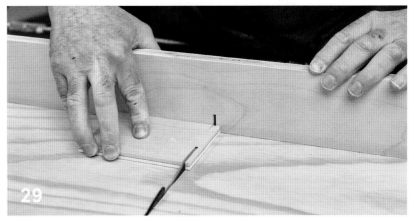

ADD SOME COLOR TO THE INSIDE

Good design considers every detail, even what a box looks like when you open it. I love a colorful surprise inside, so I use bright fabrics to line the bottom. Choose a color that complements the lid and chosen paint color for the outside, and a print that is small enough that it's repeated many times inside the box.

30 ROUGH OUT THE FABRIC. Place the bottom on the fabric. Use a rotary cutter to cut out a piece that's ⅛ – ¼ in. wider and longer than the bottom.

31 SPRAY GLUE ON THE PLYWOOD. Coat it evenly with spray adhesive (3M 77), but don't saturate it, because the glue will soak through the fabric. If it does soak through, it's visible as a stain even after it dries.

32 PRESS THE FABRIC ON. Start at one end and smooth it as you lay it down, working toward the opposite end.

33 TRIM FLUSH. Set the rotary cutter's blade against the bottom and cut around it.

PAINT THE BOX

The only paint I use is milk paint, because I love its variegated color and organic feel. I use Old Fashioned Milk Paint Co. powders, because I like the colors the company offers. The green I am using here is made by mixing one part Marigold yellow with one part Federal blue.

ADD WATER TO THE POWDER. Warm water works the best. Add 1½ parts water for every part of powder.

STIR IT UP. Use a wide piece of scrap that's around ¼ in. thick. Mash up the powder to remove any clumps, and let the mixture sit for at least 30 minutes, stirring every 5 minutes.

SAND THE BOX. Depending on the surface left by your planer, you should start at P-180 or P-220 grit, and work up to P-320 grit. Use light pressure, applying it to the side that's being sanding. Do not hold the box by the vertical sides, or by the one that's up in the air. Many a box has been broken when held that way for sanding.

BRUSH IT ON. Use a brush with Taklon bristles, wetting them before dipping the brush into the paint.

MAKE THE FIRST COAT SMOOTH. In most climates, it takes about an hour for the first coat to dry. Sand it with P-320-grit paper, using a light touch so that you don't go through the paint.

ADD A FEW MORE COATS. Brush on. Sand. Repeat until the paint is as opaque as you'd like. Personally, I apply coats until the grain is no longer visible.

GLUE IN THE BOTTOM

It's critical that the bottom fit snugly, so that there is a tight glue joint between it and the box. This strengthens the box. The bottom lifts the box slightly off the surface to create a nice shadow line and make the box visually lighter.

34

34 **SPREAD GLUE IN THE RABBETS.** Only the side of the rabbet needs glue, where the edge of the bottom contacts the rabbet.

35 **POP IN THE BOTTOM.** Press firmly to ensure that it's fully seated in the rabbet.

36 **CLAMP BETWEEN CAULS.** The key here is light pressure. Too much pressure can break the box.

35

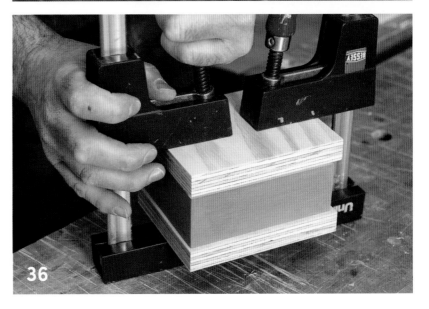

36

ADD A LID AND PULL

Quartersawn stock is the right choice for the lid, because it's stable and the straight grain works well with the box's dimensions and shape. This one is made from Western hemlock. The pull is cocobolo.

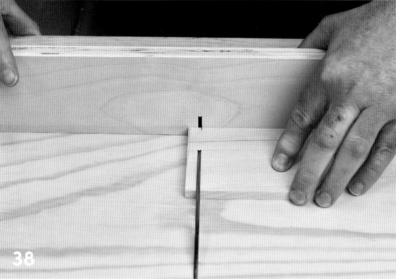

37 **RIP IT CLOSE.** Leave the lid just a bit too wide. It should just barely fit into the opening.

38 **CROSSCUT TO LENGTH.** When testing it in the box, you should be able to fit the lid and feel a little friction as it goes, but also be able to pull it back out.

39 **SHOOT TO FIT.** Start with the length, so any tearout is removed when you are fitting the width. A lid made from quartersawn stock, like this one, should have a narrow ($\frac{1}{32}$ in.) gap around all sides.

40 **SHAPE THE PULL WITH HAND TOOLS.** Start with a rasp to remove waste quickly, then move to files to tune the arc before sanding.

41 **MEASURE THE WIDTH.** Align the pull with one side of the lid, and use a rule to measure the distance from the pull to the other side of the lid. Half this distance is how far the pull should be inset from the edge.

42 **SNEAK UP ON THE CENTER.** Use a combination square or a Veritas sliding square (which is what I use) set to half the measurement you just made, to locate the pull in the lid's center.

43 **CHECK FROM BOTH SIDES.** The pull is centered when the square touches it when checked from both sides without pushing the pull farther away from the side.

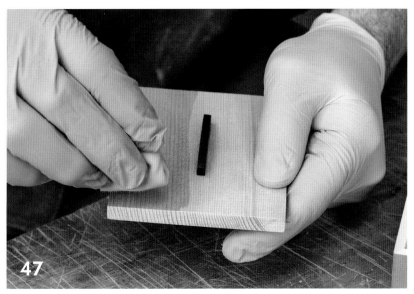

44 **LAY DOWN SOME TAPE.** Carefully stick some blue tape alongside the pull. If you bump the pull, reset it and try again.

45 **REPEAT FOR THE PULL'S LENGTH.** Use the same process to center the pull on the lid's length, and add a piece of tape.

46 **GLUE DOWN THE PULL.** A few drops of cyanoacrylate glue is all it takes. Use the blue tape to locate the pull and press it down firmly for 20 – 30 seconds.

47 **FINISH THE LID AND PULL.** Clean the pull thoroughly with denatured alcohol to remove any sanding dust, apply several coats of shellac. See p. 38 –39 for my complete finishing process.

The question that I have been asked more times than any other is probably this one: Why don't you reinforce the miter joints in your boxes with splines? Well, I don't like them. I find them unattractive, at least when they are made with a deeply contrasting wood. Fortunately for me, splines are not necessary for the type and size of miter joints in my boxes. However, before I can explain why they aren't, we need to take a quick look at the way wood moves as it gains and loses moisture.

A tree is a series of concentric layers made up of fibers that absorb moisture, but also can dry out, somewhat like a sponge. And like a sponge, when wood takes on moisture, it expands. When it dries out, it shrinks. Wood can expand and shrink along its grain, across its grain, and in thickness. Movement along its grain (i.e., a change in its length) is so minute that it's not worth worrying about, but the other two directions need to be considered. So, let's go back to the tree. The most movement occurs tangential to the grain, to those concentric layers of yearly growth. If you look at board's endgrain and the grain arcs up and back down as it goes across the board's width (if it's a "flatsawn" board, in other words), the board moves the most across its width. However, if the grain runs up and down in straight lines through the board's width, if it's a "quartersawn" board, then it moves the most through its thickness.

Here's another important fact about wood movement. The bigger the board, the more it moves. So, a 14-in.-wide flatsawn board moves much more than a 3-in.-wide flatsawn board, and a 4-in.-thick quartersawn board moves much more than a ¼-in.-thick quartersawn board.

Okay, hold that information for a moment so we can talk about miter joints. There are two types: frame and box miters. Frame miters are the type used to make, well, frames (e.g., picture frames). Box miters are the kind that join casework like the boxes in this book. With a frame miter, the joint runs diagonally across the board's width, and if the wood is flatsawn, its movement can pull the joint open as it expands and contracts. That's one reason why frame miters have the reputation for being weak.

Box miters are square to the board's width. So, if a box is made from flatsawn stock, then box sides will move the most parallel to the joint, and their movement will not tear the joint apart. If the sides are made from quartersawn stock, then they will move the most in their thickness. That would be a problem, except that box sides (well, my box sides) are thin, so they barely move, if at all, in their thickness. Wood movement isn't a problem for box miters.

Another potential source of failure in a miter joint is the glue surface. Wood fibers are a bit like drinking straws. The open end of the straw is exposed in the endgrain. When you put glue on the endgrain, the fibers begin to drink it in. In fact, so much of the glue can be pulled into the endgrain that the resulting joint is starved for glue, so it can fail. There are two ways around this. First, you can size the joints before gluing them. Make a mixture of 50 percent water and 50 percent PVA woodworking glue. Spread it on the joints and let it soak in for about 20 minutes. Then go back and apply full-strength glue to the joints and assemble the box. In my experience, the resulting joints are quite strong. The other option is to apply full-strength glue and let it set for a few minutes then apply more glue before assembling the box.

The last thing to consider is these boxes are light-duty, and they won't be handled much. So, they don't need to be engineered to withstand the racking forces of your fat uncle leaning back in his chair after eating six helpings at Thanksgiving dinner. Will one of my boxes break if you throw it against wall. Perhaps, but is that really the joints' fault? I don't think so. And you should get some help if you are throwing boxes against the wall.

Box 2

PEN & PENCIL BOX

When I'm not in the shop I like to draw robots. I use pens to draw them, and markers to color them. Because I'm bit obsessive, I quickly owned a lot of both. So, I made some boxes to hold them. I wanted them to be beautiful, but didn't want to spend a lot of time making them and fussing over grain matches at the corners. The solution: a painted body and solid wood lid without hinges. This box is nearly identical in construction to the first box. The difference between them is the cool way the lid stands up in a deep rabbet cut into the back of the box. I chose this style of lid so that I could open the box and grab a pen or marker, and not need to put the lid on my drawing surface. The box I'll show you how to make is painted Marigold yellow and has a walnut lid, but I've made it in many different paint and wood combinations. Federal blue and cherry work well together, as do slate and tiger maple, and Bayberry green and Douglas fir. I leave the top edge of the box unfinished to frame the lid. It's a way of giving focus to the beauty of the wood.

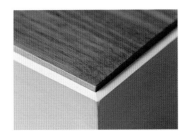  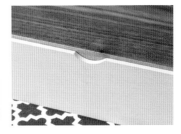

TOOLS

+ Jointer
+ Planer
+ Bandsaw
+ Tablesaw
+ Dado set
+ Block plane
+ Drill press
+ 1⅜" Forstner bit
+ Rotary cutter

MATERIALS

+ Basswood
+ Walnut
+ Plywood
+ Fabric
+ Milk paint

PARTS LIST

PART	L	W	T
Front/Back	8¾"	2⅜"	¼"
Ends	4"	2⅜"	¼"
Lid/Bottom	8⅜"	3⅝"	⅜"

DRAWING

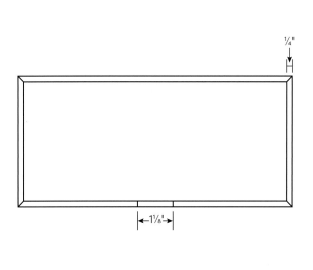

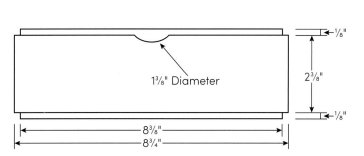

Notch Detail
Cross Section of Box Back
¼"
1⅛"
⅜"
Miter
1/16"
7/16"
¼"
1/16"
3/16"
⅛"
1⅜" Diameter
2⅜"
⅛"
8⅜"
8¾"
3⅝"
4"
3/16"

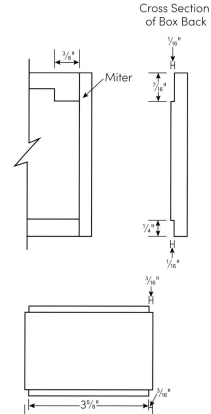

MAKE THE BOX SIDES

Basswood is great for milk paint, and left unfinished it creates a bright interior, making it ideal for this box. You can make the sides from a single board that's long enough for all four sides, plus 6 – 12 in. to account for snipe.

1 **SQUARE UP THE END.** Cut far enough in to remove any snipe created by the planer.

2 **CUT THE LONG SIDES.** Butt the square end against the stop and cut the front. Slide the board against the stop again and cut the back.

3 **ADD A SPACER FOR THE ENDS.** The stop is 4¾ in. long, the difference between the length of the sides. Press the board's square end against the stop and cut the first ends, repeat for the second end.

4 **START WITH THE NARROW RABBETS.** Set up a pair of box joint blades (they cut perfectly flat and square rabbets, unlike a dado set) and sacrificial fence for a 1/16-in.-deep by 1/4-in.-wide rabbet. Rabbet all edges except the top edge.

5 **MOVE THE FENCE.** Set it 7/16 in. from the box joint blade's outer teeth. Do not adjust the blade height.

6 **RABBET THE BACK'S TOP EDGE.** Press the side flat on the table to ensure that this second cut is at the same depth as the first cut and the rabbet is uniform in depth across its width.

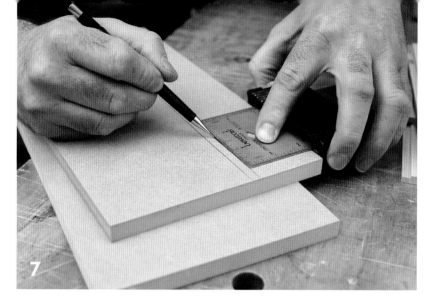

DRILL THE FINGER DIP

There's no pull on the lid. Instead, there is a small cutout in the top edge of the front. The lid's front edge is exposed just enough for you to get your thumb on it and pry it up. You can then grasp it between your thumb and forefinger until it drops into rabbet at the back.

7 **LAY OUT FOR THE BOX EDGE AND RABBET.** Mark two lines parallel to the edge of a piece of MDF. The one farthest from the edge represents the front's top edge, and the one closest to the MDF's edge is the bottom of the rabbet.

8 **MARK A CENTERLINE.** Use a combination square so that it is square to the lines you just laid out.

9 **DRAW A CIRCLE.** If you don't have a template like this one, use a compass. The circle's diameter is 1⅜ in. Its bottom should be just a hair above the line that represents the rabbet's bottom.

10 **DRILL A HOLE.** Use a Forstner bit. Although a slow speed is often recommended for large diameter bits, it's okay to run them a bit faster than suggested. The higher speed results in a smoother cut.

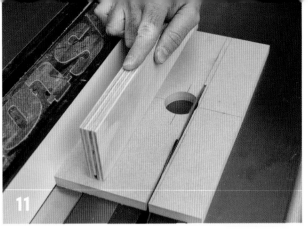

11 **RIP AWAY THE WASTE.**
Cut just to the side of the line
that represents the side's top
edge, leaving the line.

12 **TRANSFER THE
CENTERLINE.** Use a small
square to draw the line
down the hole's side.

13 **THE BASE NEEDS A
CENTERLINE, TOO.** After
placing the top layer of the
jig on the base, transfer
the centerline to the base
with a tick mark.

14 **WRAP THE LINE.** Use
a square to lay out the
centerline to the edge
of the base.

15 **ATTACH THE DRILLING
GUIDE TO THE BASE.**
Spread glue on the bottom
of the top layer. Set it
on the base, making sure
the centerlines line up,
and secure it with some
brad nails.

16 **DRILL THE RELIEF.** After
marking a centerline on
the box front, place it on jig
(rabbet facing up), aligning
its centerline with the jig's,
and drill the hole.

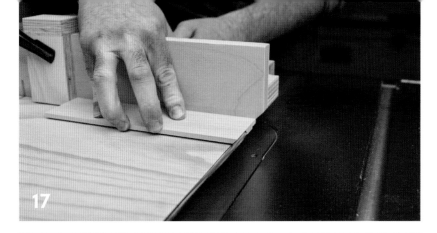

NOTCH THE SIDES TO FIT THE TOP

The deep rabbet in the back by itself is not enough for the lid to stand up, because the lid is ⅜ in. thick. There need to be small reliefs cut into the sides, too. As you open and close the lid, the corner softens and rounds over, and the lid will open and close smoothly, as if it were hinged.

17 MITER THE SIDES. Set a stop block for the front and back. After cutting their miters, add the spacer block and miter the ends.

18 LAY OUT THE NOTCH. Mark a line ⁵⁄₁₆ in. from the inside of the miter to the front of the notch.

19 MARK THE OTHER SIDE. From the side's top edge, mark a line ⁷⁄₁₆ in. to the notch's bottom.

20 CUT ACROSS THE GRAIN. Use a narrow chisel and hand pressure to make several cuts, but do stay away from the layout lines at this point.

21 **PARE THE WASTE.** Working across the grain, the waste will pop out easily. After the first bit of waste is gone, make another series of cuts across the grain then pare across the grain again. Repeat until the notch is level with the rabbet. Then pare back to the layout lines.

22 **SAND THE INSIDE FACES.** Use P-220 grit sandpaper on a flat surface, but do not press down on the sides, which can lead to the edges and corners rounding over. Repeat the process with P-320 and P-400 grit paper.

23 **SPREAD GLUE.** After taping the sides together like you did for the first box (p. 14), add glue to both sides of the miter.

24 **TAPE IT UP.** Roll up the box and secure the last joint, pulling the blue painter's tape down tightly. Check the box for square.

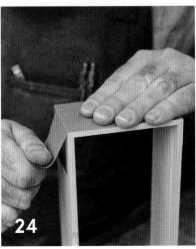

PAINT THE BOX

I'm using Marigold yellow milk paint from Old Fashioned Milk Paint Co. It's one of my favorite colors and it goes wonderfully with walnut. There's no need to tape off the top and bottom edges before you paint. Sand the outside of the box with P-220 sandpaper to prepare it for the paint.

25 BRUSH IT ON. It takes at least three coats to cover the grain completely. Sand with P-320 between coats and after the final coat.

26 CLEAN UP THE EDGE. After sanding the top and bottom edges, clean up the finger relief by hand, wrapping sandpaper around a finger and sanding lightly. Take care not to round over the edges.

27 SET THE BOTTOM INTO THE RABBET. After applying fabric to the bottom, as shown on p. 17, spread some glue in the rabbet and press the bottom into place.

28 ADD SOME PRESSURE. Sandwich the box and bottom between two cauls. Keep the pressure light, just enough to seat the bottom tightly. Too much pressure can break the box apart at the corners.

MAKE AND FIT THE LID

Because the lid is made from solid wood, you need to allow room for the lid to expand and contract across its width throughout the year. Quartersawn stock will move less, of course, but still needs some room. In the summer, you can make it a tighter fit than in the winter.

29 **CUT THE LID CLOSE.** After milling the lid to just over ⅜ in. thick, crosscut then rip it a bit larger than the width and length of the opening in the box.

30 **FIT THE LENGTH FIRST.** Trim both ends with a freshly sharpened plane. Any tearout is removed at the next step. Although wood barely moves along its length, the gaps should match those along the sides because it's more pleasing visually.

31 **SHOOT THE WIDTH.** Clean up both edges first then work from one side until the lid fits and lifts smoothly without catching the front edge of the box.

32 ADJUST THE THICKNESS. Take light shavings. The goal isn't just to prepare the surface for a finish, but also to get the lid to fit correctly in the back notch, and if it's too thin then it rattles about when standing, and might even fall out of the notch altogether.

33 CHECK THE LEAN. The lid should roll smoothly over the corner of the notch and angle slightly toward the back.

FINISH WITH SHELLAC AND WAX

Boxes are handled far less than you might think, so the finish need not be heavy. That's good because heavy finishes are unattractive. I use a very light (1 lb.) cut of shellac. It gives enough protection without looking like plastic.

WIPE ON TWO COATS. It takes just a few minutes for the first coat to dry. This will raise the grain, and the second coat minimizes the chance that you sand back to bare wood when knocking it down.

SAND IT SMOOTH. Use P-800 grit wet/dry sandpaper and a light touch. You're not trying to flatten the sides, just clean up the raised grain. Water or mineral spirits work well as lubricants and prevent the paper from clogging.

ADD A THIRD COAT. Wipe it on with the grain.

KNOCK DOWN THE SHEEN. I prefer ultra-fine steel wool, available at woodworking supply stores, to the #0000 steel wool found at home centers.

WAX CREATES LUSTER. Wax has a softer, more inviting look and feel than shellac, which is why I add a coat as the last step.

DON'T FORGET THE BOX. Although I like the matte but varied look of bare milk paint, a bit of wax makes the box more inviting to the touch and protects the paint from dirty fingers.

Box 3

A BOX WITH FLOWING GRAIN

THIS QUIET BOX CAPITALIZES on the undeniable warmth and beauty of the tight, flowing grain of old-growth Douglas fir. The grain's gentle roll and the shimmer of subtle figure dress up the clean lines and spot-on proportions. The pulls, made from cocobolo, are a point of focus without distracting from the fir's beauty. Open the box and discover the pop of a bright but charming fabric lining the bottom and lid. But what really makes this box sing is the grain as it flows uninterrupted around all four sides. It creates a quiet harmony that nonetheless says quite a bit. The technique used to create the seamless flow of grain around all four corners begins at the bandsaw, where you turn a single thick board into two thinner boards. Although you could resaw the board with a tablesaw, its thicker blade removes more wood and the resulting grain match at the corners will not be as good. Another technique you'll learn is how to keep a lid in place using just a pair of slight pulls. It's simple but clever, and never fails to impress folks when they open the box. Finally, this box is an excellent example of why proportions and grain selection are so critical to a box's success.

TOOLS

+ Jointer
+ Planer
+ Bandsaw
+ Tablesaw
+ Dado set
+ Chisels
+ Small router plane
+ Rotary cutter

MATERIALS

+ Vertical-grain Douglas fir
+ Cocobolo
+ Plywood
+ Fabric
+ Milk paint

PARTS LIST

PART	L	W	T
Front/Back	6½"	2⅜"	3/16"
Ends	3¼"	2⅜"	3/16"
Top/Bottom	6¼"	3"	¼"
Pull	1½"	¼"	⅛"

DRAWING

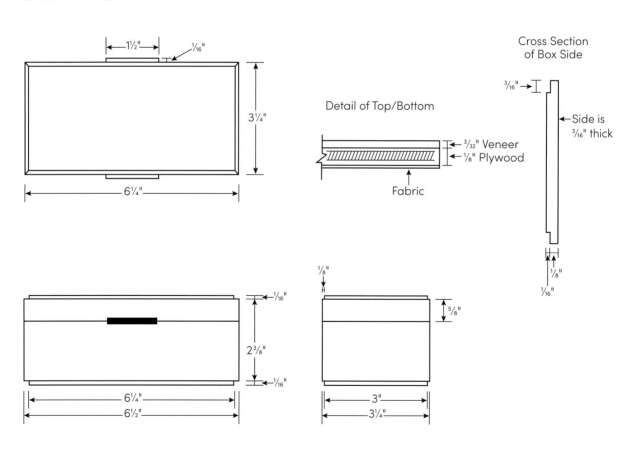

Detail of Top/Bottom
3/32" Veneer
⅛" Plywood
Fabric

Cross Section of Box Side
3/16"
Side is 3/16" thick
⅛"
1/16"

FOUR-CORNER MATCH STARTS AT THE BANDSAW

To create grain that flows around all four corners of the box, resaw a thick board into two thinner boards. This is because the corner grain match is created exactly the same way bookmatched veneer is created, except instead of using the long edge as the book's spine, you use the end of the boards as the spine. The two inside "pages" of the board become the outside of the box.

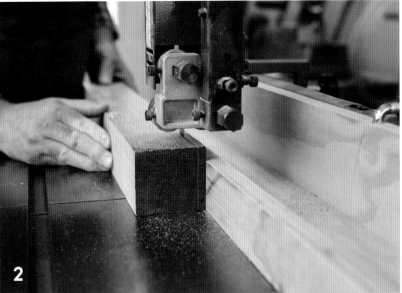

1 **JOINT A THICK BOARD.** After jointing a face and planing the board's thickness to match the height of the box sides, joint an edge square to the faces.

2 **RESAW TO MAKE A THIN BOARD.** Make it ⅛ in. thicker than the side's final thickness. If the board cups after it's cut free, there's enough meat to re-joint it (at least on a board this narrow).

3 **CUT THE SECOND THIN BOARD.** Re-joint the edge between the first and second cuts at the bandsaw. Then plane both of the new thin boards to final thickness.

4   **ROUGH CUT BLANKS TO LENGTH.** Stack the boards in the same orientation they had when part of the original thick board, and cut them at the same time, after squaring up the ends, to create two 12-in.-long boards.

5   **SAND THE INSIDE FACES.** Start with P-220 grit sandpaper and work up to P-400, using a narrow sanding block and a light touch so that the face remains flat.

6   **RABBET BOTH EDGES.** The top and bottom rabbets are identical: ⅛ in. deep by ¼ in. wide. Keep the stock pressed firmly against the fence and flat on the table to ensure uniform cuts.

7   **FINISH THE INSIDE.** Before you do this, pick which rabbets are for the bottom and do not put any finish in them. Also, make sure that the rabbets line up correctly in relation to the grain orientation on the outside of the box.

CUT THE SIDES TO LENGTH

With a rectangular box, the sides alternate long, short, long short. To create a four-corner match, you'll cut one long side and one short side from each of the two boards, but you must cut them out in the correct sequence. And, of course, for the box to have square corners, the front and back must be the same length, as must the two ends.

8 **CUT THE FIRST LONG SIDE.** Clamp a stop block to the sled's fence 6½ in. from the blade, and make the cut. Because Douglas fir is prone to chip, use a sharp blade.

9 **TRIM THE SHORT END TO LENGTH.** Set a 3¼ in. spacer block against the stop block, then slide the board against the spacer. Make the cut.

10 **MOVE TO THE SECOND BOARD.** Lay the first two sides in the exact orientation they were in before being cut. The two other sides come from the second blank.

11 **START WITH A SHORT END.** It's critical that you start from the same end of the board as you did when cutting the first long side, because that long side joins this short side when the box is assembled.

12 **CUT THE SECOND LONG SIDE.** Remove the spacer block, slide the board against the stop and trim the side to its final length.

13 **KEEP THEM ORGANIZED.** Place the second pair of sides back down on the saw table, keeping them in the same order they were in before you cut them.

14 **NUMBER THE JOINTS.** Label each side of the joint, using numbers. One joint gets 1 on both sides. The next one gets 2 on both sides, then 3, and finally 4.

15 **CUT THE MITERS.** These are cut just as the miters for the first two boxes were cut. Set the stop for the longer side, miter them, put in the spacer block, then miter the ends.

16 **GLUE UP THE BOX.** Tape the sides together (using the numbers on the outside to get them in the correct order), spread the glue, and the roll up the box. Check it for square before setting it aside to let the glue dry.

ADD THE TOP AND BOTTOM PANELS

This box's lid is cut free from the box body, but before you do that, the bottom and lid panels need to made, fit, and glued in place.

---

17 **SPICE UP THE INSIDE.** After gluing veneer to the ¼ in. plywood core and fitting the panel, glue fabric to the inside face and trim it to fit.

18 **GLUE THEM IN PLACE.** It's quicker to glue in both panels at the same time. Use cauls and do not tighten the clamps too much. All they need to do is hold the panels in place as the glue dries.

CUT THE LID FREE

The best way to separate the lid from the box body is with a bandsaw, because it cuts in a single plane and there are no steps at the corner as there usually are when you cut the lid with a tablesaw. I use a 3 - 4 variable-tooth thin-kerf blade to do the job.

19 **SAND IT SQUARE.** Slide some sandpaper under your tablesaw's rip fence. Press either the top or bottom against it and sand the box sides. The next step is much easier when the sides are square to the top and bottom.

20 **KEEP IT TIGHT TO THE FENCE.** This ensures that the cut is straight both along the length and across the box's width.

21 **CLEAN UP THE EDGES.** Sand in a circular motion. The smaller the circle the less noticeable the sanding marks are. Start with P-220, and work up to P-400.

PULLS HOLD THE LID IN PLACE

Now that the lid is cut free, it will not stay on the box without some help. For this box, I'm using two small pulls, one on the front and the other on the back. The pull is glued into a mortise in the lid, and fits into a matching mortise in the box body. When the lid is on the box, the pull is trapped by the bottom mortise, keeping the lid in place.

22 LAY OUT THE MORTISE.
After taping the lid to the box, register a combination square or sliding square against the top and draw lines for the top and bottom of the mortise. Use a square to lay out the mortise's ends.

23 SCORE ACROSS THE GRAIN. A sharp chisel and hand pressure is all it takes to cut deep enough for this shallow mortise. Make a cut about every 1/16 in. along the mortise's length.

24 CUT WITH THE GRAIN.
Carefully press a chisel, held parallel to the grain, down into the mortise. Stay just inside the layout lines.

25. **HOG OUT THE WASTE.** Lay down a narrow chisel and push it through the mortise. The waste should pop out or perhaps curl up. Either way, it comes up easily. Just take care not to dive down too deep.

26. **FLATTEN THE BOTTOM.** Use a small router plane to level the mortise' bottom. Then pare back to the layout lines with a chisel.

27. **FIT THE PULLS.** Start with the length, so that any tearout is removed when you trim the pull's width to fit.

28. **GLUE THE PULL INTO THE LID.** Use yellow glue and two small cauls. Check that the pull is tight against the top edge of the mortise and flat against the bottom.

SHELLAC AND WAX MAKE IT SHINE

Vertical grain Douglas fir is gorgeous, especially when the grain is as tight as it is on this box. The best way to bring out its beauty is a few light coats of shellac. A bit of wax on top gives it the perfect soft luster.

29 APPLY TWO COATS OF SHELLAC. Wipe on the first and let it dry, then wipe on the second. A bit of old shirt folded up works well, because it doesn't hold too much shellac, so it doesn't go on heavy.

30 GIVE THEM A SAND. After the second coat has dried for a few minutes and is no longer sticky, clean it up with some P-800 wet/dry sandpaper, using water to lubricate the surface and prevent the paper from clogging.

31 BUFF AFTER A THIRD COAT. Ultra-fine steel wool smooths the shellac and leaves a dull but uniform sheen that's ready for wax.

32 ADD LUSTER WITH WAX. I like the soft, inviting shine of Renaissance Wax. It's also nice that all you need do is wipe it on. No buffing required. However, any high-quality furniture wax will work.

When designing a box, begin with its proportions, because they are the foundation on which a beautiful box is built. And just as a successful home cannot be built without a solid foundation, a beautiful box cannot be made without good proportions. A box's length, width, and height should come together and create a harmony that sings quietly in the background. You hear it, and sense it, and it affects you, but you do not give active and conscious attention to it. When you come across a box with good proportions, you don't take conscious note of them; you sense them, you feel them, because they inform and make possible the beauty you see, but they are not surface features like wood grain, color, joinery, and pulls.

That's all fine, but the question you want answered, I'm sure, is more practical: How do I nail the proportions? Start with a proven design aid like the golden ratio or Fibonacci sequences. Both provide you with ratios that create pleasing dimensions. The key is to use them in the right way. I've found that although either system results in two dimensions, say the length and width, that are proportioned well, if you also generate the third dimension using the system the resulting box can be ungainly.

The first box I made using a Phi ruler (it has two scales on each side: one that is normal and the other either increases or decreases by the golden ratio) was spot on for its length and width, but was far too tall. It looked like a little toad. I remade the box, increasing its length and width, but made it much shorter. The second box was perfect. So, proportioning systems like the golden ratio are best taken as starting points.

Here's how I use them now. I begin by determining the proportions of the box side that will be seen the most. For the first box in this book, which sits on a table or dresser, that's the top, but for the last one, it's the front. After sketching as many possible versions as I can, altering the proportions, arrangement of drawers, compartments, lids, and pulls, I choose the one I like best and draw it on graph paper. This helps me draw the proportions accurately, and I do not worry about dimensions.

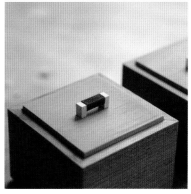

When I've got that sorted, I turn my attention to the third dimension. For boxes that sit on a table or dresser, I think shallow is best, because it's more practical. However, a deeper box works if there are trays inside. For small cabinets with drawers, depth is critical because the drawers need to be useable (6 – 7 in. deep is nice). So, my advice is to let utility and function determine the final dimension.

One last bit of advice: Good proportions are about more than the length, width, and depth/ height. They need to be carried throughout a box. The size and spacing of the grain on the sides needs to harmonize with the side's length and width. The pull should match the size of the lid or drawer front. If the interior is lined with fabric, the pattern on the fabric should be small and repeated so that it looks right. A partially seen pattern feels incomplete and unsettling. Design is in the details, and so too are proportions.

Box 4

A BOX WITH THREE COMPARTMENTS

I like bento boxes because their compartments, which often vary in size and shape, create interesting patterns or arrays of shapes. Naturally, this inspired me to make wooden boxes with multiple compartments and lids. The first one I made had two compartments and lids, and I loved it. In the years since, I've made many boxes this way. One of them even had seven compartments and lids. This box is similar in design to the first one I made, except that it has three compartments and lids instead of two. I made the box with riftsawn cherry, and the lids with quartersawn Western hemlock. Their straight grain harmonizes with the box's clean lines, and emphasize its proportions and the shapes that the compartments and lids create. When making a box with multiple lids, it's critical that their shapes, sizes, and arrangement are well balanced. I do that here by making the middle compartment twice as wide as the other two. The smaller side lids are rectangular in shape, which mirrors the shape of the box and middle lid. One more note about the box's design: The dividers have rabbets on both sides of the top edge, so they appear to be thinner than the box sides. It's a subtle difference but creates a structural hierarchy that reinforces the sense of order and pattern created by the lids.

  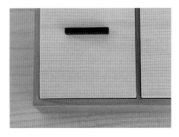

TOOLS

+ Jointer
+ Planer
+ Bandsaw
+ Tablesaw
+ Dado set
+ Router table
+ 90° V-groove bit

MATERIALS

+ Riftsawn cherry
+ Quartersawn Western hemlock
+ Cocobolo
+ Plywood
+ Fabric
+ Milk paint

PARTS LIST

PART	L	W	T
Front/Back	12"	1⅞"	¼"
Ends	4"	1⅞"	¼"
Dividers	3¾"	1⅜"	¼"
Outer Lid	2¾"	3⅝"	⅜"
Middle Lid	5⅞"	3⅝"	⅜"
Bottom	11⅝"	3⅝"	5/16"
Outer Pull	1¼"	5/16"	⅛"
Middle Pull	2¼"	5/16"	⅛"

DRAWING

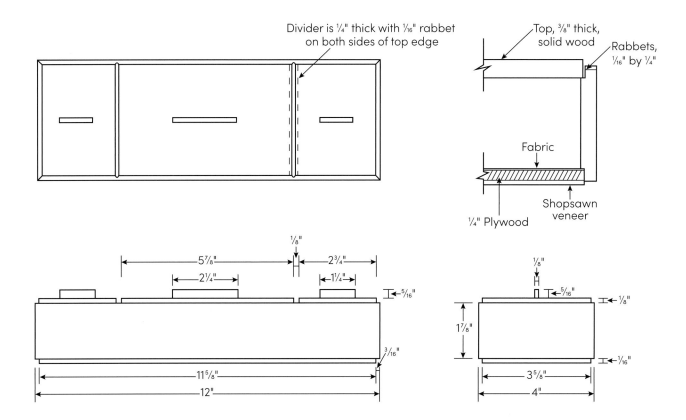

Divider is ¼" thick with 1/16" rabbet on both sides of top edge

Top, ⅜" thick, solid wood

Rabbets, 1/16" by ¼"

Fabric

¼" Plywood

Shopsawn veneer

MAKE THE BOX SIDES AND DIVIDERS

The grain on this box wraps continuously around all four corners, so make them the same way you made the sides for Box 3. However, start with blanks that are at least 12 in. longer than the final lengths of the front and one end, so that you have enough to make the two dividers.

1 **RESAW TO MAKE THE SIDES.** Joint and plane the board so that its thickness matches the sides' height. Mark one of the board's faces with a triangle so that you can keep the two new thin boards in order after you've cut them.

2 **CROSSCUT FOR THE SIDES.** Because the dividers have different rabbets than the sides, cut the dividers free now. Make certain that the boards are oriented just as they were in the original thick board before you make the cut, so that you can still create a four-corner match on the box. Plane them to final thickness.

3 **SAND THE INSIDE.** P-220 grit should be coarse enough to remove any machine marks left by planer. Then, work through P-320 and P-400 to prepare the surface for a finish.

4 **RABBET THE SIDES.** Set up a dado stack and sacrificial fence for a rabbet ⅟₁₆ in. deep by ¼ in. wide, and cut a rabbet on the inside face of the top and bottom edge.

5 **TOP EDGE OF THE DIVIDERS GETS TWO.** The rabbets in the dividers are the same size as those in the sides, but the dividers have rabbets on both faces of the top edge. There is no need to cut a rabbet into the dividers' bottom edges.

6 **FINISH THE INSIDE.** Apply several coats of shellac, following the same sequence of shellac and sanding demonstrated on p. 38 – 39. Any glue that squeezes out when the box is assembled pops off after it has dried.

7 **CUT THE FIRST LONG SIDE.** After squaring up the end of both boards used to make the sides, clamp a stop block to the sled's fence 12 in. from the blade and cut a long side.

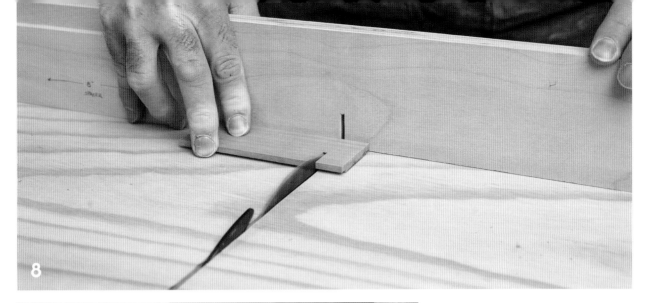

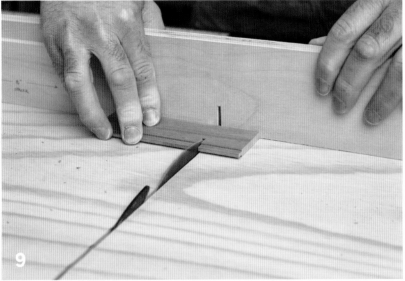

8 **TRIM THE ENDS TO LENGTH.** Add an 8 in. spacer block next to the stop block and cut both of the short ends. Remove the spacer and cut the second long side.

9 **ROUGH OUT THE DIVIDERS' LENGTH.** Put the spacer block back in place and cut two dividers. Their final length is less than the length of the box's ends, so using the spacer to cut them gets them close.

10 **MITER THE SIDES.** Use a stop block and spacer to cut 45° miters into the ends of the sides. Remember that you are not cutting the sides shorter at this stage, so set the stop block for the long sides accordingly. The spacer, butted against the stop, takes care of the box's ends.

USE A BIRDS-MOUTH FOR THE DIVIDERS

The miter joints at the box's corners create an angled line where two sides meet, a detail mirrored where the dividers join the sides. To create the joint, rout a 90° V-groove in the side, and miter both faces of the divider so that two 45° bevels meet in the middle of the divider's thickness.

---

11 **GIVE THE DIVIDER A SPEAR POINT.** Set a stop block to cut a miter across one end, then flip the divider over and cut another miter. They will meet in the center of the divider's thickness, and their shoulders will be aligned with one another.

12 **ROUT THE BIRDSMOUTH.** Chuck a 90° V-groove into a router table. After making a few test cuts to get it close to the correct depth, rout a dado 3 in. from one end of a long side. Rout into the top edge but stop before the bit comes out of the bottom. Use a wide push block to keep the side square to the fence.

13 **CHECK THE FIT.** Place the mitered end of the divider and put it into the V-groove dado. Look for the shoulders on the divider to meet the inside face of the side. If they don't come down to the face, the groove is too shallow. If they fall into the groove, the groove is too deep.

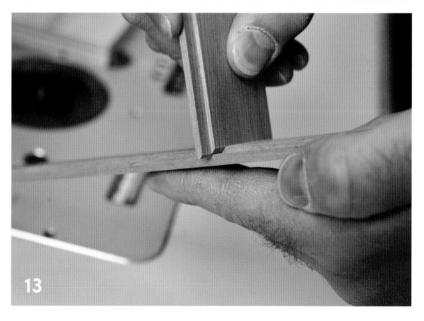

14 **DROP DOWN.** You'll need to rout from the bottom rabbet to the top rabbet for two of the V-grooves. Hold the rabbet above the bit, turn on the router, then lower the side onto the bit and push the side through. This way, you don't see the V-groove from the bottom of the box.

15 **GLUE THE JOINTS.** Tape the joints together and spread the glue.

16 **TAPE UP THE BOX.** After rolling up the box, secure the last corner with blue painter's tape, pulling tight to ensure that there is enough clamping pressure on the joint.

17 **CHECK FOR SQUARE.** The measurement across the two diagonals should be the exact same. If the box is out of square, then the dividers will be, too, and it's harder to make the lids.

18 **SPREAD GLUE FOR THE BOTTOM.** A thin coat on the wide side of rabbet is all it takes.

19 **PRESS IT IN.** Glue on the fabric to the bottom's top surface, then after seating the bottom in the rabbet, butt the box between two plywood cauls and add a few clamps. Do not use a lot of pressure, which might break the joints apart.

FIT THE DIVIDERS

The best way to ensure that there are no gaps in the birdsmouth joints is to carefully trim the divider's length while cutting the miters on the second end. A simple micro-adjust block makes it easy to get the perfect length.

20 **MITER THE DIVIDER'S SECOND END.** Use a two-part stop for these cuts. One part is a standard stop block, the other is the micro-adjust stop made from a piece of plywood and a wood screw.

21 **TEST THE FIT.** The divider will be too long at this point, but testing gives you an idea of how much shorter it needs to be.

22 **ADJUST THE STOP.** Turn the screw so that it backs out of the stop. This moves the other end closer to the blade and results in a shorter divider.

23 **TRIM THE DIVIDER.** Recut the miters at one end of the divider.

24 **SNUG BUT NOT TOO LONG.** The fit is right when there are no gaps in the joints, but the divider doesn't push out the box sides. As you get close, adjust the screw in the stop just a fraction of a turn at a time. Patience is an important tool.

25 **MARK THE HEIGHT.** Insert the divider upside down into the box. Use a sharp pencil, or a .5 mm mechanical pencil, to mark where the box's top edge meets the divider.

26 **RIP IT DOWN.** Make a push stick especially for this cut. It should be long enough to cover the entire width of the divider and sit flat on the divider.

27

28

29

27 REFINE THE HEIGHT. After testing the divider in the box, use a shooting board and plane to adjust its height. The spot to check is the bottom of the rabbets. It's critical the divider's rabbets align with those in the sides. If the top edge of the divider is still proud when they do, you can always plane it flush.

28 DON'T USE TOO MUCH GLUE. The divider absolutely will push excess glue down and out onto the fabric when you press it in.

29 DROP IN THE DIVIDER. Apply pressure at both ends, so that it does not go wonky and get stuck. Clamps are not needed if you fit its length correctly.

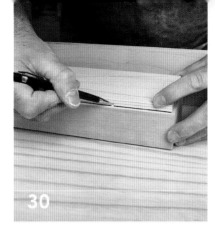

ONE BOARD, SEVERAL LIDS

Although there are three lids, it's important that they are tied together visually, so that there is a sense of unity among them. The way to achieve this is to cut them sequentially from one board. The grain flows from one lid to the next and gives a subtle visual cue that they are one even though they are not.

30 **MARK FOR THE FIRST LID.** After ripping the board close to the lids' final widths, set it on top of the box with a square end against the outside edge of the first compartment. Mark where the lid hits the divider.

31 **CUT IT FREE.** It's okay if the lid doesn't fit perfectly into the box at this point, but it should not be loose.

32 **MAKE THE MIDDLE LID.** Place the end of the blank you just cut against the next compartment. Then mark the opposite end and cut it to length.

33 **REPEAT FOR LID THREE.** The freshly cut end of the blank goes agains the divider. Mark it then cut it.

34 **FIT THE LIDS.** Start by trimming their lengths and planing their width to fit. The gaps around all four sides should be the same. A quartersawn lid like this one needs a $\frac{1}{32}$-in.-gap in the winter. In the summer, you can make it smaller.

SUBTLE PULLS COMPLETE THE BOX

This box is all about the pattern the lids create, the clean lines, and the quiet beauty of straight grain. Fancy pulls would distract from that and fight to become the box's focal point. So, keep them simple. Cocobolo is a good choice for the wood, because its rich, chocolatey brown complements both cherry and Western hemlock.

35 **GLUE THEM ON.** Use blue tape to locate the pull on the lid, and use cyanoacrylate glue to attach it. Do not use an accelerator, because this can cause the glue to become brittle, which eventually leads to failure.

36 **MAKE IT POP.** Several coats of shellac will bring out the warmth and beauty of the cherry, hemlock, and cocobolo. For the exact finishing sequence, see p. 38 – 39.

Good design is thoughtful and deliberate, and choosing wood is part of the design process, so you should not artificially impose limitations on yourself when selecting the species, or even the specific board, that you'll use to make a box. This is why I've always bristled when folks have told me that they like making boxes because it gives them a chance to use the odd cutoffs and small leftovers piled in the scrap bin. I understand where they're coming from. Boxes are small and the scraps are, too, but the wood you use to make a box is far too important to limit your options to the little chunks of wood that you've thoughtlessly chucked into a bin for the last 10 years. The wood is the heart of the box, so to speak, and affects what the box looks like, how it feels in the hand, how well it takes detail, and how much it weighs. It affects the box's beauty and appeal.

Consider the wood's color. A box made from cherry is warm and earthy. There is a whisper calling us from an older world in its muted chatoyance. The exact same design made from hard maple is bright, cool, and almost clinical. It's a shimmering artifact sent back from a future civilization. Neither is wrong, but one, or both, might not awaken the feeling and response you intend.

Other physical features of the wood are just as important. The dancing medullary rays of quartersawn white oak are beautiful, but when confined to a small space, like the side of a box, they can overpower

the rest of the box. So, if you want to use a figured wood, make sure that the figure is subtle and small, so it becomes part of the design rather than all that is seen.

Some woods, like ash, have large visible pores, which are problematic for some boxes. A small box with miter joints at the corner should have crisp lines, but large pores break up a line. So, instead of having a clean, uninterrupted line at the corner, there will be little dips and valleys where the miters meet. This would not be noticeable on a large cabinet, but is on a small box. However, a box with dovetail joinery at the corners can handle the large pores of ash, because the visual difference between face and endgrain makes the little dips into the pores less noticeable.

Think about the wood you'll use. Consider how its color, grain, and pore structure will interact with the design. Chose a species and board that will complement rather than struggle with it.

Box 5

BOX WITH LINER & SPLINES

There is no better combination of milk paint and wood than Slate blue and tiger maple, especially if the figure is super tight and iridescent. But the combination is a bit too cool (in terms of its color temperature) for me, so whenever I pair them I accent them with a warmer wood, like the gonçalo alves splines glued into this box's miter joints. Splines are generally used to reinforce miters, but a small box like this one doesn't need them, so the reason I am using them is aesthetic. They add some warmth and provide a small counterweight to the visual impact of the slate blue milk paint and tiger maple. To prevent them from making too strong a statement, I've kept them quite thin by cutting the notches with a dozuki rather than a tablesaw blade. There is a basswood liner inside the box to keep the lid in place. And although you could leave crisp corners on mating edges of the box and lid so that the seam between disappears when the box is closed, a slight chamfer reveals the basswood, creating a delicate but bright line that's the perfect detail to finish the box.

 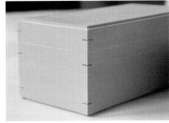 

TOOLS

+ Jointer
+ Planer
+ Bandsaw
+ Tablesaw
+ Dado set
+ Crosscut dozuki
+ Rotary cutter

MATERIALS

+ Basswood
+ Tiger maple veneer
+ Gonçalo alves
+ Plywood
+ Fabric
+ Milk paint

PARTS LIST

PART	L	W	T
Front/Back	7"	2¾"	³⁄₁₆"
Ends	3½"	2¾"	³⁄₁₆"
Top/Bottom	6¾"	3¼"	⁵⁄₃₂"
Liner F/B	6⅝"	1¹⁵⁄₁₆"	⅛"
Liner Ends	3⅛"	1¹⁵⁄₁₆"	⅛"

DRAWING

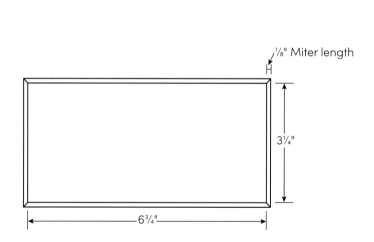

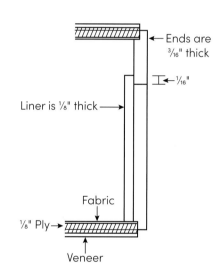

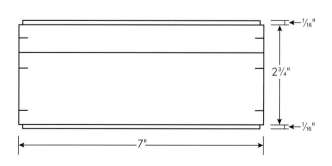

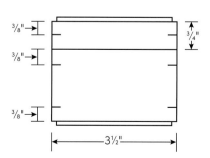

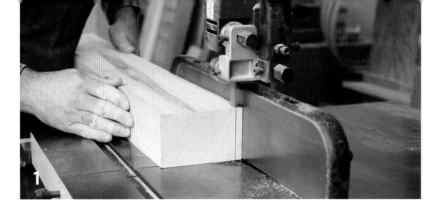

MAKE THE BOX

Like the first two boxes, this one is painted, so don't worry about matching the grain at all four corners. Instead, cut the four sides from a single piece of basswood. Do not finish the inside of the box before you glue it up, so that you can glue in the liner.

---

1 **MILL STOCK FOR THE SIDES.** Create a board that's ¼ in. thick, 2¾ in. wide and at least 24 in. long. I am using edge grain from a 12/4 basswood board, because it's quartersawn and more stable than flatsawn stock, but it's not necessary.

2 **RABBET THE EDGES.** Sand the inside face of the board to P-320 grit, and then set up your tablesaw to cut a ⅛-in.-deep by ¼-in.-wide rabbet, burying part of a dado set (or finger joint set) in a sacrificial fence.

3 **USE A STOP BLOCK FOR THE FRONT AND BACK.** Clamp it to the sled's fence 7 in. from the blade. It doesn't quite touch the sled's base so that sawdust slides under it rather than get trapped against it, which can result in one side be shorter than the other.

4 **ADD A SPACER.** This effectively moves the stop block 3½ in. closer to the blade, so that you can cut the two short ends.

5 **CUT THE ENDS TO LENGTH.** Press the board's square end against the spacer and make the cut. Slide the board against the spacer again and cut the second end to length.

6 **JOIN THE CORNERS WITH MITERS.** Set up the sled with a stop block to miter the box's front and back. Then add the spacer and miter the ends.

7 **GLUE UP THE BOX.** Use the same technique shown for the previous boxes: Tape the sides together, spread glue in the joints, roll up the box, and tape the last joint together tightly.

8 **SAND IT SMOOTH.** Because this box is painted, there is no need to sand beyond P-220 grit, but it is important for the sides to be flat. Use a light touch so that you do not round over the corners and edges.

GLUE UP THE TOP AND BOTTOM

The panels glued into the box to create the bottom and top are a sandwich with plywood in the middle and fabric on the inside face. The outside face is store-bought tiger maple veneer. I've found that's the easiest and most cost-effective way to get stunning figure. But it is more delicate than shopsawn veneer, so handle it with care.

9 **SPREAD GLUE ON THE PLYWOOD.** Cover the entire surface with a thin, even coat of standard PVA woodworking glue. Never put glue on veneer, because it will quickly curl up.

10 **TAPE DOWN THE VENEER.** Use a painter's tape that releases easily, and tape all four corners. This prevents the veneer from curling up and from sliding out of position under clamping pressure. I use a piece of veneer that's just a bit longer and wider than the plywood.

11 **ADD SOME PRESSURE.** Put both the top and bottom between a pair of ¾ in. plywood cauls that are ¼ in. longer and wider than the plywood and veneer. Use as many clamps as you can, and check that the veneer is tight to the plywood around all four edges.

12 **TRIM THE VENEER FLUSH.** Press a sharp plane blade against the plywood and press down. Work around all four edges.

13 **RIP TO WIDTH.** Cut one edge clean, mark the width directly from the box, then rip at the mark. Because tiger maple tears out easily, make small adjustments to the fence and rip again if the top is too wide rather than use a hand plane and shooting board.

14 **CUT TO LENGTH.** After cutting one end square to the sides, mark the top's length. Set up a micro-adjust stop on a sled and cut the top. Adjust the stop until the top fits in snugly with no gaps. Repeat the entire process for the bottom.

USE PAINT TO ENHANCE THE DESIGN

The edges of the lid and bottom panels are painted to cover the plywood edge, but also to create a visual boundary between them and the box. The boundary is needed because the tiger maple and basswood are so close in color, but not the same color, which looks like a mistake. Adding the milk paint shows clear design intention.

15 **TAPE PROTECTS THE VENEER.** Lay a narrow piece of painter's tape down so that it extends past the edge of the veneer and at both ends.

16 **CUT IT FLUSH.** Use a knife, pressed against the top's edge, to cut away the tape that overhangs the veneer. Then turn the top over and press the tape down around the edges to ensure that it is tight against the veneer.

17 **REPEAT FOR THE LONG EDGES.** Again, lay the tape down so that it overhangs along the edge and at both ends, then cut it flush with a knife.

18

18 **USE A NARROW BRUSH ON THE EDGES.** A ¼ in. flat brush with Taklon bristles works best, and you can find one at art supply and craft stores. Sand after the first coat then add a second. Do not add any more, because the top might not fit in the box then. Seriously.

19 **PAINT THE BOX, TOO.** Sand after the first coat with P-320 sandpaper. Brush on a second coat then sand. Add more coats, sanding between them, until the paint covers the wood completely.

19

ADD SPLINES TO THE CORNERS

The primary reason to add splines to the miter joints of this box is decorative. Their color and the pattern of their layout adds visual interest to the otherwise monochromatic box sides. They are made from goncalo alves, which is not as dark as cocobolo. Its lighter brown is a better match for the cool tones of the milk paint and tiger maple.

20 **TAPE THE CORNERS.** Use a light-color tape so that it's easier to see the layout lines you're about to make, and align the edge of the tape with the box's corner.

21 **LAY OUT WHERE THE SPLINES GO.** Use a combination square to draw a line ¼ in. from and parallel to the corner on all sides of the box. Then mark the location for every spline with a single, thin pencil line. Be sure to account for the kerf (see step 32) between the lid and box body.

22 **KEEP THE KERF THIN.** A dozuki with 20 or more teeth per inch cuts cleanly and will not damage the paint.

23 **PULL OFF THE TAPE.** After it's removed, check in the kerfs to make sure no tape is stuck in them.

24 **MAKE A REALLY THIN BOARD.** Set the fence for a cut just thicker than the kerf's width. Feed a piece of ¼ in. MDF into the bandsaw's blade to create a zero clearance surface, then rip a strip from a gonçalo alves turning blank.

25 **SAND IT TO FIT.** Press gently with your fingers so that you sand evenly. Test the fit often to avoid making the board too thin.

26 **CUT THE SPLINES WITH A HANDSAW.** After ripping the board into narrow strips, stack them and cut 12 spline blanks, plus several extra in case one or a few break when you are gluing them in or trimming them.

27 **PUT GLUE IN THE KERF.** A scrap of veneer is thin enough to get glue inside the kerf without also getting it all over the surrounding paint.

28

29

30

28 **TAP IN THE SPLINES.** Do not hit them hard. They will break. If one does break, cut it out with the dozuki and try again.

29 **CUT OFF THE EXCESS.** Let the glue dry for 10–15 minutes. Press down on the saw's spine to keep the teeth off the box's surface and work carefully.

30 **PARE FLUSH.** Press the chisel flat onto the box side and push the chisel in a diagonal motion across it. Do not cut straight out, because the spline's grain will break and the corner will not be sharp. If you do tear out the corner, cut out the spline with the dozuki and glue in a new one.

CUT THE LID FREE

Because it cuts through the entire box at once, the bandsaw creates edges on the lid and box that are in a single plane and mate perfectly, even if it is slightly out of square. After a bit of sanding, the box closes up without hinting that it has been cut in two.

31 ADD FABRIC TO THE TOP AND BOTTOM. Choose one with a color that complements the Slate milk paint and a small, oft-repeated pattern. Use spray adhesive to glue it on and a rotary cutter to trim it flush.

32 GLUE THEM INTO THE BOX. Spread pressure by re-using the cauls used when gluing the veneer to the plywood. Go easy on the pressure, though. Even small clamps can apply enough to break the joints apart.

33 SUPPORT THE BOTTOM. After setting the bandsaw's fence to cut the lid free, slide a piece of MDF into the blade. This prevents tearout, which would remove paint, on the bottom.

34 SAND THE CUT EDGES. Use a granite surface plate or other flat surface (like a jointer bed). Start with P-220 and go to P-320. Basswood doesn't show sanding marks from P-320 if you use a tight circular motion.

FIT THE LINER

The main purpose of the liner is to keep the lid in place, and it need rise above the box sides just ⅛ in. to do the job. Mitered corners, unlike butt joints, lock all four pieces into place, keeping them tight against the box sides.

35 **MARK DIRECTLY FROM THE BOX.** After squaring one end, place it against the inside of the box and mark the other end with a small pencil tick in line with the inside face of the box side.

36 **CROSSCUT THE LINER.** Leave the pencil line. At this point the liner should be long, so don't worry about cutting right at the line.

37 **TEST THE FIT.** This gives you a sense of how much shorter the liner needs to be.

38 **ADJUST THE STOP.** It's best to make small changes to the screw. A quarter turn is a good start, unless your liner is ⅛ in. or more too long. If that's the case, back the screw out a half turn. Cut the liner again. Test the fit. Repeat until it slides in with hand pressure and there are no gaps. Check to see if it fits the other side. If it does, cut the second liner. If not, make the second one to fit the second side.

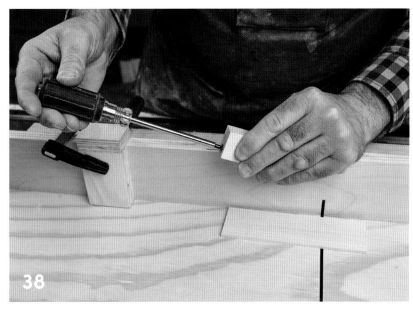

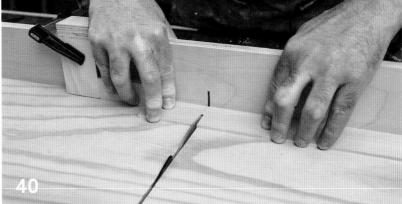

39 NOW MARK THE ENDS.
The short ends are made the
same way as the long sides.
Start by marking the length
directly from the box.

40 TRIM TO FIT. The ends,
like the sides, should slide in
with just hand pressure and
there should be no gaps in
the corners.

41 CUT THE MITERS. Start
with the long sides, mitering
them just as you did the box
sides. When you set up for
the ends, use a micro-adjust
stop block.

42 SLID THE LONG SIDES IN.
They should stay in place on
their own. If they fall into the
box, they are too short and
you'll need to remake them.

43 TEST THE ENDS. Do not
press them all the way in,
because you will not get
them back out without
damaging them or
the box. Most likely, they
will be too tight. Make a
small adjustment to the
mirco-adjust stop and
recut one end.

44 **GLUE FOR THE FRONT AND BACK LINERS.** Make sure not to spread glue on the portion of the liner that sticks above the box sides.

45 **GIVE THEM THE CLAMPS.** Leave them under pressure for about 15 minutes, which is long enough for the glue to take hold.

46 **THE ENDS LOCK IT IN.** There is no need to use glue, because the ends are too short to warp away from the box.

47 **BRING OUT THE BEAUTY.** After sanding the tiger maple to at least P-400, apply shellac, sanding with P-800 paper between coats.

48 **FINISH THE MILK PAINT, TOO.** The only time I use shellac on milk paint is when it's unavoidable (milk paint, like shellac, is a top coat). Because the splines need to be finished, you've got to hit the milk paint with shellac, too. It makes the paint a bit darker, but it still looks great.

Box 6

BOXES ON A TRAY

This box is what happens when a guy who loves bento boxes meets Judson Beaumont, a furniture designer and maker who lived in Vancouver, British Columbia. One of the things Jud was known for is his playfulness: a dresser that is shaped like a black dress and hangs on the wall. It's a little black dresser. He also made cabinets that look as if they've exploded into multiple pieces, with each piece containing a drawer or two. It's those cabinets that inspired me to group a pair of small boxes on a tray. I've made many variations on the idea since then, but this one is my favorite. I love that something so simple—a square box—can be repeated and arranged in such a way as to create something beautiful and functional. The tray is critical, because it allows you to determine how the boxes are arranged. In this case that's in a straight line with uniform spacing between them. Without the tray, which has shallow mortises that register the boxes, they can be set down randomly, which would destroy the harmony that the orderly arrangement creates. Another feature that contributes to the harmony is the walnut's tight, straight grain. It not only wraps continuously around each individual box, but flows continuously around all three boxes taken as a group. The day I figured out how to do this was one of my best days in the shop ever. I'll show you how to do.

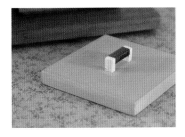  

TOOLS

+ Jointer
+ Planer
+ Bandsaw
+ Tablesaw
+ Dado set
+ Small plunge router
+ ½" Dado clean out bit
+ Rotary cutter

MATERIALS

+ Walnut
+ Basswood
+ Plywood
+ Fabric
+ Milk paint
+ Embroidery thread

PARTS LIST

PART	L	W	T
Front/Back	2⅝"	1¹⁵⁄₁₆"	³⁄₁₆"
Ends	2⅝"	1¹⁵⁄₁₆"	³⁄₁₆"
Lid	2⅜"	2⅜"	⁵⁄₁₆"
Bottom	2⅜"	2⅜"	³⁄₈"
Tray	10⅞"	4⅛"	³⁄₈"

DRAWING

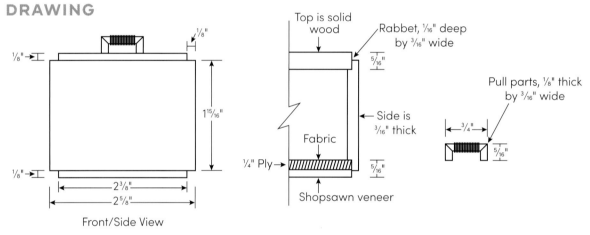

Front/Side View

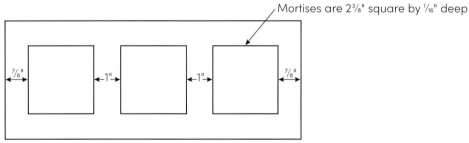

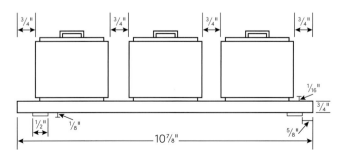

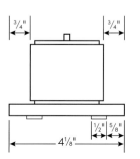

THE GRAIN WRAPS AROUND ALL THREE BOXES

Grain that wraps around not just three boxes individually but also around the boxes taken as a group is mind-blowing, at least until you learn that the technique used to create this double wrap is just a variation on the technique used to wrap the grain around a single box.

1 **RESAW FOR THE FOUR-CORNER MATCH.** You need two boards after resawing, and each one should be long enough to cut six box sides from it, plus another 6-8 inches to accommodate planer snipe.

2 **CUT THE RABBETS.** Set up a dado set and sacrificial fence to cut a ⅛-in.-deep by ³⁄₁₆-in.-wide rabbet along both edges of the boards. Make sure you cut them on what will become the inside of the boxes.

3 **FINISH THE INSIDE.** It's much easier to finish two long boards than 12 short box sides, especially if the miters have been cut. Use the process shown on pp. 38 - 39.

4 **SQUARE THE END.** Stack the two boards together as they were before being resawn, and align their ends. Cut away enough to remove any planer snipe.

5 CUT TWO AT ONCE.
Because the boxes are square, all the sides are the same length, and you need just one stop block setup to cut them.

6 REPEAT FOR ALL THE SIDES. Cut a total of six pairs of sides, placing them down on the saw's table or the sled in order as you cut them. It's hard to keep so many parts arranged correctly.

7 LABEL THE JOINTS.
The two mating sides of the first joint are marked "1" and "1." Those for the last joint on the third box are marked "12" and "12." Using sequential numbers makes it easier to keep the sides of each box individually organized, and all three boxes organized as a group.

8 CUT SOME MITERS. There are a lot to cut, but because the sides are all the same length, you need just one stop. Use a hold down to keep your fingers away from the blade.

9 GLUE UP THE BOXES.
Blue painter's tape holds the joints together and applies clamping pressure. Spread the glue on both sides of the joint, roll up the box, then tape the last joint closed. Any squeezeout pops off easily because the inside has been finished.

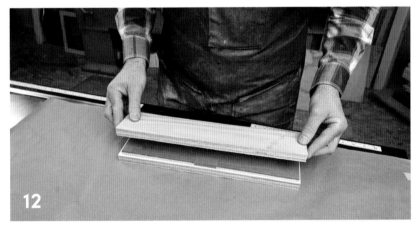

FABRIC BRINGS COLOR INSIDE

These bottoms are made like all the other bottoms so far. There's a plywood core with shopsawn veneer on the bottom and fabric on top. Choose a fabric that complements the walnut, has a small a pattern that's repeated and is bright enough to lighten the box's interior.

10 **START WITH A SINGLE PIECE OF PLYWOOD.** Spread a thin coat of PVA wood glue over a 3¼-in.-wide by 12-in.-long piece of ¼ in. plywood, making sure to cover all the way to the edges.

11 **ADD THE VENEER.** Cut to the same dimensions as the plywood, align the veneer with the plywood's edge and tape the two together so that the veneer doesn't twist out of alignment under clamping pressure.

12 **SANDWICH BETWEEN CAULS.** Made from ¾ in. plywood that's ¼ in. oversize in length and width, the cauls spread pressure evenly, ensuring that the veneer is glued tightly to the plywood all the way out to the edges.

13 **BRING THE PRESSURE.** Big parallel jaw clamps like these apply pressure over a wide area, so four is enough. If you use F-style clamps, use as many as you can, because they apply less pressure over a small area.

14 **RIP TO WIDTH.** After cleaning one edge and marking the width directly from one of the boxes, cut the blank's opposite edge. Check to see how it fits. If it's too wide, nudge the rip fence closer to the blade and trim the blank.

15 **CROSSCUT TO LENGTH.** Use a micro-adjust stop with the screw extended a bit, and do not remove it after cutting the sides. You'll need it when you make the template used for the tray.

16 **GLUE IN THE BOTTOMS.** Attach the fabric with spray adhesive, and cut it flush with a rotary trimmer before gluing the bottom in place. Do not apply too much pressure with the clamps, because that can break the joints.

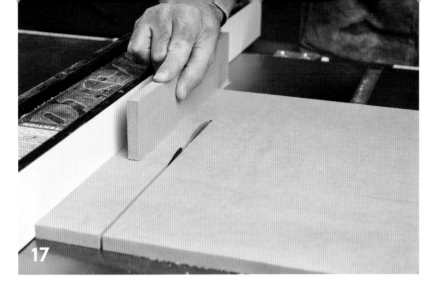

MAKE A TEMPLATE FOR THE TRAY

The most efficient way to create the shallow mortises for the boxes is routing them. A template provides accuracy, allowing you to rout all three mortises in quick succession. You'll need a ½ in. mortising bit with a ½ in. guide bearing, which you can find at woodworking supply stores and online.

17 **RIP A STRIP FOR THE CENTER.** It should be just a bit wider than the box bottoms.

18 **ADJUST THE STOP.** The stop and micro-adjust are still set up from when you crosscut the bottoms to fit the boxes. Turn the screw into the micro-adjust. After adjusting it, the micro-adjust should be ⅟₃₂ in. farther from the blade.

19 **CUT THE LENGTH.** Place the strip of MDF against the micro-adjust and cut a piece free.

20 **ROTATE AND CUT THE WIDTH.** Turn the piece of MDF 90° and place it against the micro-adjust stop. Trim it to width. You now have a square piece of MDF that is ⅟₃₂ in. longer and wider than the box bottoms. This spacer is used to locate parts when gluing the template together.

21 MAKE THE SPACERS. These small pieces—you need two of them—sit between the three open spaces in the template and determine the distance between the boxes when the sit in the tray.

22 GLUE ON AN END PIECE. Cyanoacrylate is the best glue to use, because it dries quickly. Hand pressure suffices to secure the end piece to the template's side.

23 LOCATE THE FIRST NARROW DIVIDER. Put the spacer against the middle end piece that you just glued into place. Put a few drops of cyanoacrylate glue on the end of the narrow divider. Butt it against the spacer and press it firmly against the template's side. Hold it there for 20 or so seconds.

24 ADD THE SECOND END. After using the spacer to locate and glue on the second narrow divider, use the spacer to locate the second end piece. Glue it to the template's side with cyanoacrylate glue.

25 CLAMP THE TEMPLATE TOGETHER. After applying some cyanoacrylate glue to the open end of all the middle piece's, put the second side on the template and clamp it all together. Although the glue dries quickly, I have found it best to let the template sit for 30 minutes before you complete it.

26 **CUT THE ENDS FLUSH.**
Is it necessary for the template's function? No. Is the template neater, and so more satisfying, with the ends flush? Yes. And that's a good thing.

27 **LAY OUT FOR THE RAILS.**
Attached to the bottom of the template, the four rails locate the tray so that the mortises are routed in exactly the right spots. These layout lines indicate where the inside edge of each rail should fall.

28 **GLUE AND NAIL THEM TO THE TEMPLATE.**
I prefer PVA glue for this joint because it's stronger than cyanoacrylate glue, and because you can secure them with brad nails until the glue dries, there's no advantage to cyanoacrylate's shorter drying time.

29 **ADD RAILS AT BOTH ENDS.**
These are the same width as the tray. You can use the same rip fence setting to rip the tray and piece of MDF to width after making these two pieces.

HOW TO LOCATE THE BOXES ON THE TRAY

A big part of why this set of boxes is so pleasing is that they are spaced uniformly and are oriented square to one another. Although you could set them on the tray's surface and come close, it's better to set the box bottoms in shallow mortises, which guarantees that they will always be spaced and oriented properly.

30 **MARK THE TRAY'S LENGTH.** After ripping a blank to width and squaring one end, place the blank in the template and mark the second end directly from the template.

31 **PRESS IT INTO THE TEMPLATE.** Cut the tray to length. Check its fit. Too long? Trim it and try again. After it fits snugly, push it down between the rails, making sure that it's flat against the bottom of the template.

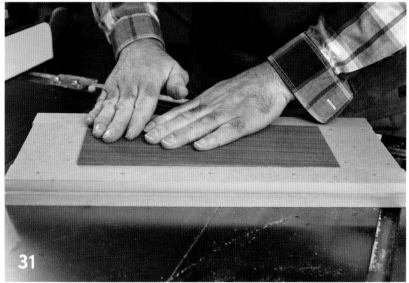

32 **USE AN MDF BACKER.** This piece was ripped to width at the same time as the tray blank. Cut it to length using the same stop block used when cutting the tray to length. Press it into the template. You need this because the tray is thinner than the MDF rails, and without it the tray would be pushed down by the router bit when you try to plunge into it.

33 **PLUNGE THE BIT TO THE TRAY.** This is the first step in setting the bit's cutting depth. It should come to rest on top of the tray.

34 **ADJUST THE DEPTH STOP.** The mortises should be around 1/16 in. deep, which is the thickness of this rule. Place the rule between the turret and plunge stop. Lock the plunge stop at this setting.

35 **ROUT THE MORTISE.** Slowly plunge the bit to its cutting depth to avoid a cutting mark that's deeper than the rest of the routing you'll do. Go around the perimeter first then clean out the middle.

36 SQUARE THE CORNERS.
Hold a chisel's back tight against the template and push down. There's so little material here that you can remove it in a single pass.

37 CLEAN UP THE BOTTOMS.
A router never leaves a clean and truly flat bottom, so sand the mortise bottoms by hand. Start with P-220 paper and work up to P-400.

38 ADD FEET. Because it would be nearly impossible to clamp these without them moving under the pressure, use cyanoacrylate glue to secure them rather than PVA glue.

39

40

41

42

THREAD-WRAPPED PULLS TOP THE BOXES

The technique I used to cover my pulls with thread is borrowed from fly fishing. It's how the line guides are attached to the rod. Because these pulls are small, it can be challenging, but don't give up. I have huge farmer hands and I can still manage to get it done.

39 **FIT THE LIDS.** With a micro-adjust stop, you can dial in the length and width of each top at the tablesaw, but don't hesitate to do the same with a plane and shooting board.

40 **POP THEM WITH PAINT.** I'm using Old Fashioned Milk Paint Co. Marigold paint. It looks amazing when paired with walnut.

41 **PARE ANGLES FOR THE PULLS.** You need two different paring guides: 90° and 45°. They don't need to be as fancy as mine, but should have a stop so that all the legs are the same length and the all the top bars are the same length. Please do not try this with a tablesaw. The parts are far too small for such foolishness.

42 **GLUE THEM TOGETHER.** This is just like gluing up the boxes, but there are only three sides. Leave a tail on the blue tape that's long enough to reach across the open long side and stick down to the opposite leg.

43 START THE WRAP. Lay the one end of a piece of embroidery thread down on the underside of the pull and pinch it into the corner. Wrap the thread around the pull and over the section that is laid down. Continue to wrap it around the pull and over the laid-down section.

44 WORK ACROSS THE PULL. Keep each turn of the wrap tight against the one that came before it and cover the entire length of thread under the wrap.

45 WRAP OVER A LOOP. Fold a loose piece of thread into a loop and lay it down on the underside of the pull so that the closed end is facing the unwrapped end of the pull and the loose end extends back toward the other leg. Wrap the thread over the loop until you reach the second leg and have covered the entire pull.

46 THREAD THE LOOSE END THROUGH. If the wrapping thread is too long, clip it shorter and slip the loose end into the loop.

47 PULL THE LOOP UNDER THE WRAP. Pinch the loop and loose end of the wrapping thread with one hand so that the wrap doesn't get sloppy, and pull the open end of the loop with your other hand until both the loop and wrapping thread have gone under and back out of the wrap.

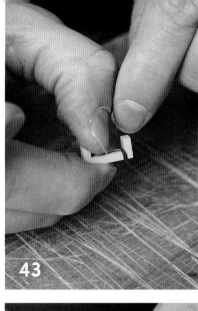

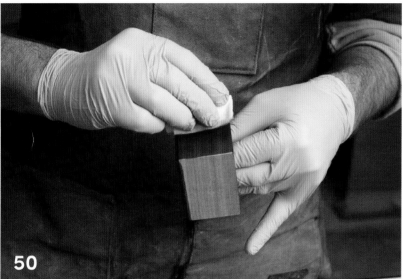

48 TRIM THE EXCESS. Use sharp scissors, like these little fly-tying scissors. Their delicate size lets me get close to the wrap, but be careful not to cut into the wrap, because it will unravel.

49 GLUE THE PULL TO THE LID. A drop of cyanoacrylate glue on the bottom of each leg is enough. Why not PVA glue? There's just no good (i.e., that doesn't require cumbersome cauls) way to clamp the pull while the glues dries.

50 SHELLAC THE BOXES. Three coats should do it. Be sure to sand between them with P-800 wet/dry paper, and use an ultra-fine steel wool after the last coat. Then wax.

51 WAX THE LIDS. Give some care to keep wax off the pull, but the truth is that after the wax dries it no longer darkens the wood, so it's no big deal if a bit gets on a leg or even the thread.

Box 7

AN ELEGANT TEA BOX

I designed and made this tea box for a young woodworker who wanted one of my tea boxes. I really didn't want to make a traditional tea box, and after some time doodling ideas in a sketchbook, I settled on this design. What makes it work, I think, is that I left out two drawers to create an open space. What's it for? Well, you can store a bottle of honey there like the young woodworker does, or display a favorite piece of (narrow) pottery, like the tea cup you see in the photo. Although it is important for the boxes and furniture you make to be functional, don't forget the furniture has meaning and purpose beyond its utility. Part of that purpose is to be beautiful and bring joy into our lives. That's what I was thinking about when I eliminated the two drawers and left a space for a favorite tea cup. This cabinet is a step (or two, or maybe even four) up from the previous boxes in terms of the challenge it poses, because both the case and the drawers are joined with dovetails. However, I'll show you the smartest and most efficient way I know to cut them. Spoiler alert: It's not with your gaffer's bag of hand tools. Drawers can be tricky, too, but I'll explain how I make and fit them. It's a technique that almost completely eliminates the need to "fit" the drawers to the opening.

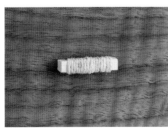

TOOLS

- Jointer
- Planer
- Bandsaw
- Tablesaw
- Miter Gauge
- Dado set
- Combination blade ground for dovetails
- Router table
- Rabbeting bit
- Spiral downcut bits (¹⁄₈" and ¹³⁄₁₆")

MATERIALS

- Walnut
- Basswood
- Plywood
- Fabric
- Milk paint
- Hemp twine

PARTS LIST

PART	L	W	T
Base Legs	2¹⁄₃"	6¹⁄₂"	³⁄₈"
Base Top	7¹⁄₂"	6¹⁄₂"	³⁄₈"
Cabinet T/B	7¹⁄₂"	6¹⁄₂"	³⁄₈"
Cabinet Sides	11¹⁄₂"	6¹⁄₂"	³⁄₈"
Vert. divider	11	6⁵⁄₁₆"	¹⁄₄"
Horz. Dividers	3³⁄₈"	6⁵⁄₁₆"	¹⁄₈"
Spacer	6³⁄₈"	³⁄₈"	³⁄₈"
Drawer Fronts	3¹⁄₄"	3¹⁄₂"	¹⁄₄"
Drawer Sides	5⁷⁄₈"	3³⁄₈"	¹⁄₄"
Drawer Backs	3¹⁄₄"	3³⁄₈"	¹⁄₄"
Drawer Bottoms	2¹⁵⁄₁₆"	5¹¹⁄₁₆"	¹⁄₈"
Liner T/B	3¹⁄₄"	6³⁄₁₆"	¹⁄₈"
Liner Sides	6⁷⁄₈"	6³⁄₁₆"	¹⁄₈"
Back Panel	11¹⁄₄"	7¹⁄₄"	³⁄₁₆"

DRAWING

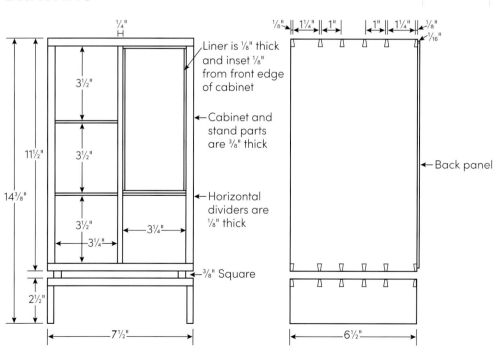

Liner is ¹⁄₈" thick and inset ¹⁄₈" from front edge of cabinet

Cabinet and stand parts are ³⁄₈" thick

Horizontal dividers are ¹⁄₈" thick

³⁄₈" Square

Back panel

DRAWING

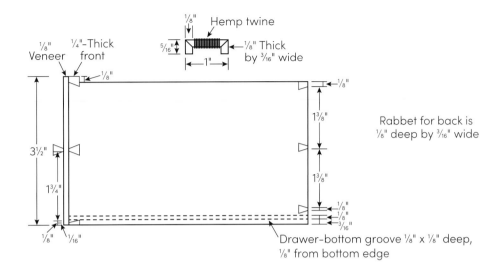

$\frac{1}{8}$"
Veneer | $\frac{1}{4}$"-Thick front

$\frac{1}{8}$" | Hemp twine

$\frac{5}{16}$" | $\frac{1}{8}$" Thick by $\frac{3}{16}$" wide

1"

$\frac{1}{8}$"

$3\frac{1}{2}$"

$1\frac{3}{4}$"

$1\frac{3}{8}$"

$1\frac{3}{8}$"

$\frac{1}{8}$"

Rabbet for back is $\frac{1}{8}$" deep by $\frac{3}{16}$" wide

$\frac{1}{8}$"
$\frac{1}{8}$"
$\frac{3}{16}$"

$\frac{1}{8}$" | $\frac{1}{16}$"

Drawer-bottom groove $\frac{1}{8}$" x $\frac{1}{8}$" deep, $\frac{1}{8}$" from bottom edge

WRAP THE GRAIN UP, OVER, AND BACK DOWN THE CASE

Although the base is separate from the cabinet, they are quite close to one another, and it looks more harmonious and pleasing if the walnut's grain runs continuously across the gap then wraps around the cabinet and back down the other side. Use a single board for this run, and another board for the top of the base and the cabinet's bottom.

1 **CUT ONE OF THE LEGS.**
The stop block is set to cut the cabinet side, but a spacer block acts as a temporary stop for the base's legs. Make sure to square up the end of the board first.

2 **A CABINET SIDE COMES NEXT.** After removing the spacer, slide the board against the stop and cut the side to length. Place it down next to the leg in the same orientation they were in when still part of the board. The cabinet's vertical divider should be cut with one end against the stop, too.

3 **THE CABINET TOP IS THIRD.** A second spacer effectively moves the stop closer to the blade.

4 **NO SPACER NEEDED FOR THE NEXT PART.** Now you are cutting the second cabinet side, and the end of the board goes against the stop.

5 **A SECOND LEG TO STAND ON.** Place the long spacer back against the stop and cut the second leg free from the board.

6 **KEEP THE PARTS ORDERED.** Lay the legs and cabinet parts on your saw in the same orientation they were in before being cut. I use an arrow across each joint, all of them pointing in the same direction, as a visual reminder of how they should be oriented in the cabinet.

DOVETAILS JOIN THE CORNERS

There's no stronger joint for casework than the through dovetail. I cut them with my tablesaw, because I can easily create a symmetrical layout, and those in the base align perfectly with those in the case. Although I use a specially ground blade, any tablesaw blade works. Of course, you can always use a different technique and set of tools.

7 **SET THE GAUGE.** I aim to have my tails and pins flush after assembly, so I set the blade to just cover the board's thickness. Also, I prefer a cutting gauge, because nothing severs the grain like its knife when sharp.

8 **SCORE THE GRAIN.** Take a few light passes across the board.

9 **MARK THE VERTICAL DIVIDER, TOO.** This is a great trick, because the scribed line clearly identifies where to cut the shoulder later, when you are fitting the divider into the assembled cabinet.

10 **LAY OUT THE TAILS.** My bevel gauge is set to match the angle at which my tablesaw blade is tilted when I cut the tails (10°). And like any civilized and rational human being, I cut the tails first.

11 **MAKE THE FIRST CUT.** Tilt the blade to match the tail's slope, and clamp a stop to the sled so that the blade cuts to the outer layout line.

12 **SCOOTCH THE BOARD.** This second cut removes the remaining waste for the half-pin socket on the board's edge. Repeat this process for all four half-pin sockets on the cabinet side, then do the same for the other cabinet side and the base's two legs.

13 **MOVE THE STOP.** Make the second tail cut. Flip the cabinet over and make the same cut on the other edge. Rotate it end for end and make the same two cuts on the opposite end of the cabinet side.

14 **REPEAT TO COMPLETE THE TAILS.** Move the stop again for the next cut down the line. Remember that you make four cuts at each stop position (two on each end of the cabinet side).

15   **POP OUT THE WASTE.** There should be just a small triangle left, but if you use a standard tablesaw blade, you'll need to clean out the corners, too.

16   **TRANSFER THE TAILS.** After aligning the tail board on the endgrain of the pin board, use a mechanical pencil (or a marking knife if you must) to trace the tails onto the endgrain. Transfer the lines down the outside face of the parts.

17   **SET UP FOR THE PINS.** I use a set of box joint blades, set for a ⅜-in.-wide cut, to remove waste between the pins. The sled, which is attached to a miter gauge, is angled to match the slope of the tails. Only one side of the pin is cut now.

18   **CUT THE FIRST SIDE OF THE PIN.** Line up the layout line with the zero-clearance kerf in the jig's base and cut to the side of the line. This is important if you used pencil to transfer the tails: Leave the pencil line. You can make more than one cut now, but be careful not to cut into the pin at the other side of the tail socket.

19 **SWITCH IT UP.** Move the miter gauge to the other miter slot, and angle it in the opposite direction. I also move the jig so that I get a clean kerf so that I know exactly where to put my layout lines when cutting the second side of the pin.

20 **COMPLETE THE PINS.** The first cut should define the second side of the pin. You can then quickly remove the remaining waste.

21 **FIT THE JOINT.** If you take care when transferring the tails and cutting the pins, it's possible for the joint to fit right from the saw, but if it doesn't, pare carefully with a sharp chisel until the tails fit between the pins with little more than hand pressure.

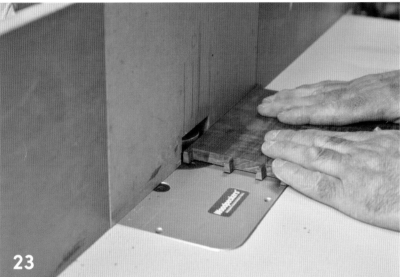

ROUT DADOES AND GLUE UP THE CABINET

I try to keep construction simple for little cases like this one. All of the dadoes are ⅛ in. wide and cut with a spiral bit in the router table. They are stopped dadoes, so you'll need to stop the cut before going out the front for some of them, and for the rest you need to lower the part onto the bit to start the cut. Cut the dadoes in the vertical divider at the same time you rout them in the cabinet sides.

22 **STRAIGHT IN FROM THE BACK.** A push block helps keep the cabinet top (and bottom) square to the fence during the cut. Pencil lines on the fence are located ³⁄₁₆ in. before and after the bit. For this cut, the line in front of the bit shows where to stop the cut. The one after the bit shows where to align the cabinet parts for cuts that start on the front edge, which you do not want to rout through.

23 **CUT THE RABBETS.** These are stopped at both ends, so ease the cabinet parts onto the bit inside of the pins (or tails) then stop before cutting into them at the other end.

24 **GLUE IT UP.** The cheeks of the pins are the most important place to put glue, because their long grain glues well to the long gain of the tails' cheeks.

25 **SOME LIGHT TAPPING REQUIRED.** The water in the glue will expand the wood and even if you had the joint fitting just right, it can be a bit too tight after the glue goes on. Use a caul to spread the blow's pressure and prevent any dents.

26 **CLAMPS THE JOINTS.** After ensuring that the joints are fully seated, I take off the clamps and make sure that the cabinet is square, then set it aside for the glue to dry. This is unorthodox, but I've found that a good-fitting joint will stay nice and tight.

27 **GLUE UP THE BASE, TOO.** This one is tricky, because there isn't a fourth side to help keep the legs square to the top. Use clamps to close the joints and then remove them. Check that they are square after taking off the clamps.

28 **SQUARE UP THE RABBET.** Begin with light paring down into the rabbet, then pare across the grain the remove the waste. Repeat this process to work down to the rabbet's inside edge.

29

29 CLEAN UP THE CABINET AND BASE. Plane and sand the cabinet and base to prepare them for finishing.

30

30 GLUE THE SPACERS TO THE BASE. Apply glue only to the front half of the spacer. This allows the base to expand and contract toward the back of the base.

31

31 JUST A BIT OF INSET. Use a combination square or other adjustable square to locate the spacer $1/16$ in. from the front edge.

ADD THE DIVIDERS

The biggest challenge when fitting the dividers is the notches needed so that they slide past the stopped end of the dado. I'll admit that it's something I struggle with at times. The scribed shoulder line on the vertical divider makes its notches easier, and if you sharpen your pencil to a point before marking the horizontal dividers, your accuracy will greatly improve.

32 **RABBET BOTH SIDES.** Set the router table's fence so that a rabbeting bit cuts to the scribed shoulder line. Set the bit's height lower than you think it needs to be. Rout a rabbet on both faces of the vertical divider. Test to see if the tongue fits in the dado. Raise the bit a little and recut both rabbets. Repeat until the tongue fits snugly.

33 **TRIM THE TONGUE.** The exact length doesn't matter, so you can cut it a little short. What really matters is that the shoulder-to-shoulder distance matches the same distance on the cabinet's sides, which it does because the divider was the same length as the sides, and you laid out identical shoulders on all three pieces.

34 **CHECK THE FIT.** The divider should slide in using ony hand pressure. If it's tight, take a shaving from both sides of the tongue, so that it remains centered.

35

36

37

35 **NOTCH THE FRONT EDGE.**
Remove the first $\frac{3}{16}$ in. of
the tongue so that the
divider slides up past the
stopped dado and comes
flush with the cabinet's front
edge. Rip down the grain
with a dozuki then pare
the waste with a chisel. It's
okay if it comes out past
the cabinet, too, because
you can plane it down to
match. Rip the divider to
width (take material from the
back edge) so that it doesn't
stick into the rabbet for the
cabinet back.

36 **ROUGH OUT THE
HORIZONTAL DIVIDERS.**
They should be just a bit long
at this point. Cut them from
a board that's been milled
to fit snugly into the dadoes,
which are $\frac{1}{8}$ in. wide.

37 **PLANE TO FIT.** Use a
shooting board and block
plane to shorten the divider
until it fits into the cabinet.
Check that it does not push
the vertical divider out
of plumb.

38 **MARK FOR THE NOTCH.** Use a .05 mm mechanical pencil to draw a line on the divider, with the pencil lead tight against the vertical divider (and cabinet side for the other side of the divider). Cut the notch with a small dozuki and chisel.

39 **GLUE IN THE VERTICAL DIVIDER.** Do not put glue all the way to front of the dado, because as you push in the divider, it pushes the glue to the front.

40 **SLIDE THE HORIZONTAL DIVIDERS INTO PLACE.** It's important that they are flush with the cabinet and vertical divider, because planing them flush afterward is challenging. The plane will tear out the grain on the cabinet and vertical divider.

38 **GIVE 'EM THE CLAMPS, BOSS.** A plywood caul both protects the spacers and spreads the pressure evenly.

39 **THE CABINET IS GLUED TO THE SPACERS, TOO.** Again, glue goes only on the front half of the spacer to accommodate wood movement and to force the movement to the back of the cabinet, which keeps the front edges aligned.

40 **LINE THEM UP.** Press a piece of plywood against the front edge of the base then push the cabinet against the plywood. Do the same on one side as well.

41 **BE GENTLE WITH THE CLAMPS.** You definitely need pressure to create a strong and durable bond, but you don't want the cabinet to shift out of position. Check it with the plywood after the clamps are on and adjust if needed.

DOVETAILED DRAWERS ON THE QUICK

There's no denying the beauty of a drawer with half-blind dovetails, but they are a pain to make, especially when the drawers are as small as the ones in this cabinet. That's why I started to make through dovetails at the front of the drawer and then glue a veneer to the drawer front to create the look the of half-blind dovetails. You get the beauty without the fuss.

45 **CUT THE DRAWER-BOTTOM GROOVE.** Use a standard-kerf 24-tooth rip blade with teeth that have a flat-top grind, so that the groove has a flat bottom.

46 **CROSSCUT THE SIDES.** Cut them in pairs to speed things up a bit, and use a stop to ensure they are all the same length.

47 **MAKE THE FRONTS AND BACKS.** At this point they should all be square and the same length, but after cutting them organize them in pairs: one front and one back per pair.

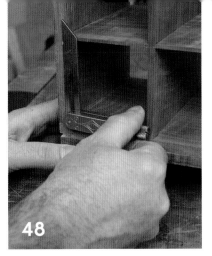

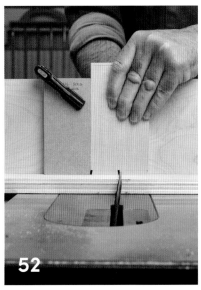

48 SET A BEVEL GAUGE. The cabinet is most likely a bit out of square, and the drawer front should be fit to match, so use a bevel gauge to capture the angle of the cabinet. Do this for both sides of the drawer pocket.

49 TRANSFER TO THE DRAWER FRONT. Place the body of the gauge against the front's bottom edge and trace the blade's angle onto the front.

50 SHOOT THE LINE. Shim out the end of the front with some blue painter's tape or a business card so that the layout line is parallel to the plane's travel then shoot the endgrain until you reach the line.

51 CHECK THE POCKET. After shooting both ends of the drawer front, put it into the pocket to see how it fits. At this point, it should just barely fit into the pocket. I normally shoot the top edge parallel to the top of the pocket at this point, and leave a small gap, about ⅟₃₂ in., between the drawer's top edge and the pocket.

52 CUT THE DOVETAILS. I use the same tablesaw technique I used for the cabinet joinery, but use whichever dovetail method you are most comfortable with.

53 **ASSEMBLE THE DRAWER BOXES.** Make sure that they are square after glue up. Then let the glue dry for several hours before continuing the fitting process.

54 **PLANE THE SIDES.** The drawers are probably a bit tight in the pockets at this point, so set up a block plane for a light shaving and take a few passes over each side. However, it's critical that you not change the angle of the front's endgrain when you do this, so that the drawers remain parallel to the sides of the pocket.

55 **SMOOTH OPERATION.** It should take just a handful of passes with the plane for the drawer to fit properly. Look for the drawer to slide smoothly—do not force it—without binding or dragging on the case. If it's tight, turn the cabinet around and look in from the back to see where you need to remove material.

56 **FLATTEN THE FRONT.** There are two things to keep in mind here. First, the drawer front should be flush to the sides' endgrain. Second, it must be flat, so check along its length and across its width to make sure there are no low or high spots.

VENEER CREATES HALF-BLIND DOVETAILS

Because this cabinet is delicate, I use shopsawn veneers that are just over ⅛ in. thick. Use riftsawn material for its straight grain, and let it run across the bottom two drawers. The straight grain also makes it easier to match the middle and top drawer with the drawer beneath it so that it appears as if they were cut from a wide board.

62 **SPREAD THE GLUE.** A thin coat is ideal, and the glue should cover the front completely, all the way out to the edges. Because this is a flat surface, PVA glue is fine.

63 **ADD THE VENEER.** I cut it so that it overhangs the drawer front 1/16 in. on all four sides.

64 **TAPE IT IN PLACE.** Use 2-in.-wide blue painter's tape to secure the veneer to the drawer, which prevents it from twisting out of place when you apply clamping pressure.

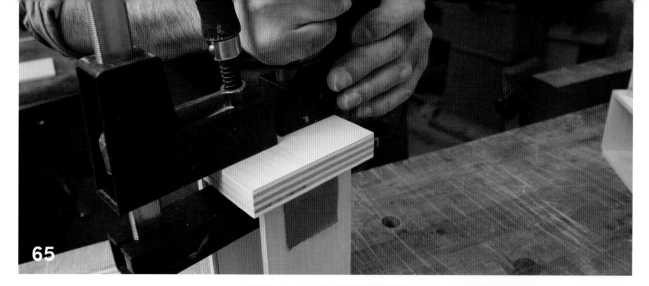

65 APPLY THE CLAMPS. Use a caul to spread pressure over the entire front. Take a look at the glue line to ensure that the veneer is tight to the drawer front all the way around.

66 ROUT FLUSH. Start on the endgrain and work your way around. I've found that some flush-trim bits don't actually rout the veneer flush, so you might need to plane or scrape the front flush after routing away most of the waste.

67 SLIDE IN THE BOTTOM. It's ⅛ in. thick to match the drawer-bottom groove. I glue the bottom into the groove in the drawer front, because the back is too thin for a screw. Pulls, liner, and back complete the cabinet Good design is about the details, so give just as much care to making the pulls, the liner, and the back as you have to the rest of the cabinet. I make the liner from basswood, but the back is ¼ in. plywood. I paint both faces and the edges of the plywood.

68

69

70

68 **MAKE THE PULLS.** Except for the dimensions of the parts, these pulls are just like those used for the three boxes on a tray and you make them the same way (see pp. 99–101). Start by gluing the pull legs in place.

69 **WRAP THE PULLS.** A thin hemp twine is a great match for the warm, chocolaty brown of the walnut. You can find it online. Get the thinnest twine you can, because it makes it easier to pull the loose end back under the wrap.

70 **PAINT THE BACK AND LINER.** Here's the recipe for the milk paint: 1½ tablespoons of Marigold, 1½ tablespoons of Federal blue, and 1 tablespoon of Snow White. Glue in the liner and then the back.

Interlude:
PAY ATTENTION TO GRAIN LINES

Boxes are made up of shapes. The sides are most likely rectangles. The lid is probably one, too, or perhaps a square. The wood grain that runs across it can either complement the shape of the box's parts, or it can struggle against it. Take a look at the Douglas fir box on p. 40. The grain runs straight and parallel to the long edge of the box sides. This enhances the rectangular shape of the sides and the box as a whole. Now imagine that instead of straight grain, there were loose, flowing cathedral grain lines. The undulating, irregular grain would fight against the rectilinear lines of the box side. I suppose my choice of words, "enhance" and "fight against," betray my preference, but I prefer the subtle beauty of the straight grain. However, even if you prefer more

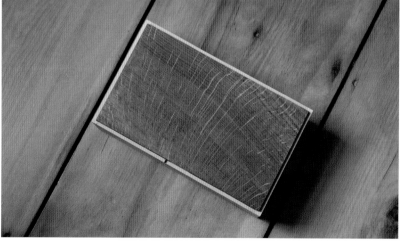

dramatic grain, you should still consider how the flow of grain lines works with the shape of a box's parts.

Yet, it's not just the flow or shape of the grain that's important. Grain tightness is critical, too. That Douglas fir box is small, and if there were just a few grain lines visible on a side, it would look odd, as if I had used a randomly selected piece of a giant board to make it. However, with many grain lines tight against one another, the side looks right because they are proportional to the side's size. The same considerations should be given to figured woods as well. Tight figure works better on small parts than loose figure, because it communicates itself more clearly.

The good thing about boxes is that they are small, so it's possible to make the small boards with the grain you want from the bigger boards you find at the lumber yard. I often find boards with straight grain that doesn't run parallel to the edge cut by the sawyer. So, I recut the board's edge to run parallel to the grain. And if the grain I want is in the center of the board, I cut the board apart so that I can get access to it. The sawmill doesn't know what you are making, and there is no need to adhere to its notion of how a board should be cut. After all, it's far more likely that the board was cut for the sake of expediency and profit than beauty, grain, and color. It would be amazing to start with an uncut boule and cut it up to create boards perfectly suited for your work, but that's not feasible. The next best thing is to realize that the lumber you buy is just a raw material and that you are not constrained by the edges cut by the sawyer.

Box 8

A BOX WITH FINGER JOINTS

This box grew out of my extreme dislike of box (aka, finger) joints. I had always seen the joint cut so that the fingers on both mating pieces were the same width and spaced uniformly. It's a layout that screams mechanization and industrialization. And it's an ugly joint. But many years ago I had an idea: Space the joint like I would dovetails, which would give the joint a less industrial look. To my surprise, the joint not only looked less industrial, it looked quite nice. So, I started to play around with it. I've since used it for box corners and drawers. I think finger joints look great in this box. There is something about the warm tones of the spruce sides and English brown oak veneers that softens the joint's industrial edge over and above what the dovetail-style spacing does. The joint also is subtle enough not to compete with the spectacular figure of the brown oak veneer I chose for the lid. The joints fade into the background, letting the medullary rays sparkle all the more. I chose vertical grain spruce for the box body because its color, when shellacked, complements the brown oak, and the tight straight grain flows harmoniously with the straight-fingered joinery. The green milk paint around the edge of the lid and bottom accentuate the box's lines and colors.

TOOLS

+ Jointer
+ Planer
+ Bandsaw
+ Tablesaw
+ Dado set
+ Router table
+ Rabbetting bit
+ Chisels

MATERIALS

+ Quartersawn spruce
+ English brown oak veneer
+ Plywood
+ Fabric
+ Milk paint

PARTS LIST

PART	L	W	T
Front/Back	10"	3"	$5/16$"
Ends	6"	3"	$5/16$"
Top/Bottom	$9\,5/8$"	$5\,5/8$"	$7/16$"
Liner F/B	$9\,3/8$"	$2\,1/8$"	$3/16$"
Liner End	$5\,3/8$"	$2\,1/8$"	$3/16$"
Linder Divider	$5\,1/8$"	$2\,1/8$"	$1/8$"

DRAWING

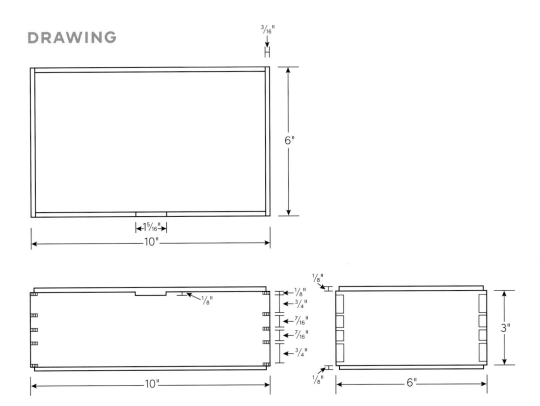

DRAWING

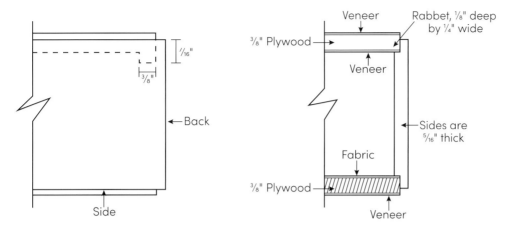

Veneer — Rabbet, ⅛" deep by ¼" wide

⅜" Plywood →

Veneer

⁷⁄₁₆"

⅜"

← Back

Side

Fabric

Sides are ⁵⁄₁₆" thick

⅜" Plywood →

Veneer

1

2

BOX JOINT WITH A MODERN TWIST

The fingers on the front and back of the box are wide, but not uniform in size, giving them the feel of handmade joinery, which they actually are, because I made them with my hands. But don't cut them with hand tools! Use your tablesaw, and keep their primary advantage over other joints: the speed at which they can be cut.

1 **SET THE GAUGE.** The cutting knife should be just shy of the opposite face. How much? Less than ¹⁄₆₄ in.

2 **SCRIBE THE SHOULDERS.** Cut both faces at both ends of the side, but not the edges. Take a few light passes to sever the fibers cleanly. This minimizes tearout when cutting the joinery at the tablesaw.

3 **LAY OUT THE JOINT.** The narrow notches are ⅛ in. wide, which matches the kerf of the blade used to cut the finger joints. Because the joinery is cut at the tablesaw using a sled and stop block, you need lay out just one end of one box side.

4 **FIND THE CENTER.** Lay a rule diagonally across the box side, so that "zero" is at the top corner and a whole number falls on the opposite edge. Find the middle between the two numbers and mark it on the box side.

5 **LAY OUT THE LAST NOTCH.** After transferring the mid-point to the side's end, make a tick mark on either side, ¹⁄₁₆ in. from the center.

6 **CUT THE FIRST NOTCH.** Use a blade with a flat top grind, and set a stop so that the blade cuts its full width. The blade height is set to cut to the shoulder. After the first cut, flip the board and make another cut on the opposite edge, then rotate the board end for end and repeat.

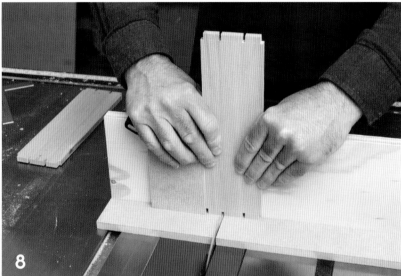

7 **ADJUST THE STOP.** Set it so that the blade cuts the second notch in from the edge.

8 **ONE STOP, FOUR NOTCHES.** After flipping the board to cut a second notch in the first end, rotate the board 180° and cut two notches in the opposite end, too.

9 **MOVE THE STOP ONE LAST TIME.** Cut the middle notch at both ends of the box side.

TRANSFER THE FINGERS AND CUT MATING SOCKETS

This is just like transferring tails to the pin board when making a dovetail joint, and you'll go about it the same way.

10 **MARK BOTH SIDES OF THE NOTCH.** A .05 mm mechanical pencil is thin enough to fit into the opening and make a clean line.

11 **CARRY THE LINES DOWN.** Because of how the side stands on the sled, you cannot see the transfer lines on the endgrain, so use a square to transfer them onto the outside face.

12 **CLEAN OUT THE WASTE.** Leave the pencil line on either side of the socket, then clean out the waste with a series of cuts. The sled is zero-clearance so this is easier than you might guess.

13 **ROUT THE RABBETS.** All of the rabbets are stopped, so start and end them between the shoulder lines. As was the case with Box 2, the rabbet in the top edge of the back is wider than the others.

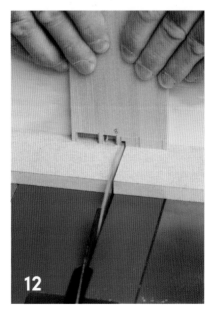

MAKE THE LID STAY

Take a look back at the second box in this book for a more detailed explanation of how to put the notch at the back of the sides that the lid stands in when opened. It's a nifty way to have a hinged lid that doesn't use hinges.

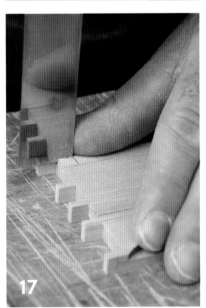

14 **LAY OUT THE NOTCH.** It's ¼ in. wide and ⁵⁄₁₆ in. long (measured from where the miter starts on the side's face). Use a small combination or double square and make sure that the lines are square to the side's edges.

15 **CUT THE FINGER.** This is the best way to ensure that you do not accidentally break off the finger as you clean out the notch. Make the cut just above the shoulder.

16 **SEVER THE ENDGRAIN.** Gently press a chisel into the notch just inside the pencil line. Do not attempt to go full depth at this point. The chisel will push itself back and over the layout line.

17 **GENTLY CUT WITH THE GRAIN.** Work your way from the open side to the layout line, leaving about ¹⁄₃₂ in. between cuts.

18 **POP OUT THE WASTE.** Work slowly across the grain with a chisel just wide enough to cover the notch in a single pass. Do not remove all of the waste at once.

GLUE THE BOX TOGETHER

The most important thing to remember is that the joint needs to be clamped in both directions to ensure that there are no gaps along the shoulder line.

19 GO EASY WITH THE JOINTS. Spruce is delicate, and the fingers are, too. After spreading glue in the wide sockets, press the joint together with your hand.

20 SPREAD THE FORCE. If you do need more than just hand pressure, use a block of plywood that covers the entire joint to protect the spruce from dents, and to spread pressure evenly.

21 CLAMP IT UP. Keep an eye on the sides. Too much pressure can bow them, and bring the box out of square. The goal is to close the joints without screwing anything up.

22

23

24

22 **CLAMP IT BOTH WAYS.** This pulls both parts of the joint tight to the shoulder and closes any small gaps.

23 **DOUBLE CHECK.** After using clamps to close the joints from both directions, remove them and measure the diagonals. If the box is square, set it aside and let the glue dry overnight. There is no need for clamps if the joints remain closed on their own.

24 **SQUARE THE RABBETS.** After the glue is dry, carefully remove waste from the ends of the stopped rabbets. I use a piece of plywood as a backer so that my chisel doesn't break through the thin rabbet wall.

FIT THE BOTTOM AND LID

Both are made from plywood and veneer. The bottom has fabric on its top face, but the lid gets veneer of both faces.

25 **RIP THE BOTTOM TO WIDTH.** Face the veneered side up, so that the blade's teeth do not tear out the veneer as they leave the cut on the underside.

26 **TEST THE FIT.** The bottom should fit snugly, but not stress the joints or push the sides out.

27 **CUT TO LENGTH.** After squaring up one end and marking the bottom directly from the box, crosscut the opposite end, making small adjustments to its length until the bottom just fits into the rabbet.

28 **SUPPORT THE TOP.** Because there is veneer on both faces of the top, place a piece of MDF beneath it when ripping it to width. Do this both when cleaning up the first edge and when cutting the opposite edge to fit the width.

31 **CROSSCUT THE TOP.** Use the same piece of MDF to create a zero-clearance "sled" beneath the top, and prevent tearout on the bottom face.

30 **NOTCH THE BOX FRONT.** Use a flat-top-grind blade, set for a ⅛-in.-deep cut, to make the finger relief that allows you to grasp the lid and open it.

31 **PAINT THE EDGES.** Tape off the veneer on the box top and bottom, making sure that the tape is tight against the veneer at the edge. Because commercially made veneer can be extremely thin, you might sand through it trying to remove any paint that seeps under loose tape.

SPRUCE UP THE INSIDE WITH TWO COMPARTMENTS

The interior of this box is somewhat big. This much space can be difficult to utilize because your knickknacks and notions tend to move about all willy nilly. Add a divider and things become manageable.

32 MARK THE LINERS FOR LENGTH. Square up the opposite end first and then do your best "eye ball measurement" to get them in the ballpark.

33 USE A MICRO-ADJUST FOR THE CUT. Clamp a stop to the sled's fence and then put the micro-adjust against it. Cut the liner at the pencil line.

34 ADJUST IN SMALL INCREMENTS. After testing the liner's fit, turn the screw slightly out, put the micro-adjust against the stop and trim the liner. Repeat this process until the liner slides into the box.

35 MITER THE ENDS. Use the micro-adjust for these cuts, too, because even though you were spot on when cutting the liners to fit, they are still too long. You can sneak up on the prefect fit with subtle turn of the screw. After the miters are cut, use a blade with a flat top grind to cut the dadoes.

36 SHELLAC EVERYTHING.
There is no way to keep it off the milk paint, so just jump in and finish it. Use the same process demonstrated on pp. 38 – 39.

37 INSERT THE FRONT AND BACK LINER. There is no need to glue the long sides in, because the divider will prevent them from bowing out.

38 SLIP THE SHORT ENDS IN. Press both ends evenly to prevent binding. If the liner does not seat fully with hand pressure, tap it in with a mallet or hammer, using a piece of wood that covers most of the top edge to prevent denting.

39 ONE BECOMES TWO. Mill the divider to match the width of the dadoes and cut it to length. You can sneak up on the length with a shooting board or a micro-adjust stop on a crosscut sled.

Box 9

A MODERN JEWELRY BOX

There is something about a set of boxes stacked atop one another that I really like. I suppose it's the geometry created by grouping individual boxes into a pattern. It's far more interesting than a square case with rows of drawers created by dividers. And I like the wink in the direction of Japanese tansu storage cabinetry. This box was inspired by a tea cabinet I made in 2016. It had the same combination of a shorter box sitting above a longer one, but also has a plinth with kumiko in it. This cabinet sits atop a simple "foot" that matches the spacer between the two boxes. These are mitered boxes, and not too challenging to make. Yes, they are deep, but the techniques used to make them are no different than the ones used to make the other mitered boxes in this book. I think it's more important to focus on the grain. It runs up the left side of the two boxes, over the top box, and down the right side of the top box. It also flows across the top of the bottom box and down its right side. Although craftsmanship is critical, never overlook the importance of choosing the right wood for a box. This entire box is made from a single piece of figured cherry. The uniformity in color, grain, and figure helps to unify the two boxes, creating a harmonious one from two individuals.

TOOLS

+ Jointer
+ Planer
+ Bandsaw
+ Tablesaw
+ Rip blade with flat top grind
+ Dado set
+ Router table
+ $3/16$" Spiral downcut bit

MATERIALS

+ Cherry
+ Basswood
+ Plywood
+ Chiyogami paper
+ Milk paint
+ Embroidery thread

PARTS LIST

PART	L	W	T
Lower Box T/B	15"	7"	$5/16$"
Lower Box Ends	$2 5/8$"	7"	$5/16$"
Lower Box Divider	$2 1/4$"	$6 11/16$"	$1/4$"
Upper Box T/B	10"	7"	$5/16$"
Upper Box End	$2 5/8$"	7"	$5/16$"
Lower Left Drawer Front	$9 7/16$"	2"	$1/4$"
Lower Left Drawer Back	$9 7/16$"	$1 1/2$"	$1/4$"
Lower Left Drawer Bottom	$9 3/16$"	$6 1/16$"	$1/8$"
Lower Right Drawer Front	$4 11/16$"	2"	$1/4$"
Lower Right Drawer Back	$4 11/16$"	$1 1/2$"	$1/4$"
Lower Right Drawer Bottom	$4 7/16$"	$6 1/16$"	$1/8$"
Upper Drawer Front	$9 3/8$"	2"	$1/4$"
Upper Drawer Back	$9 3/8$"	$1 1/2$"	$1/4$"
Upper Drawer Bottom	$9 1/8$"	$6 1/16$"	$1/8$"
Drawer Sides	$6 1/4$"	$1 7/8$"	$1/4$"

DRAWING

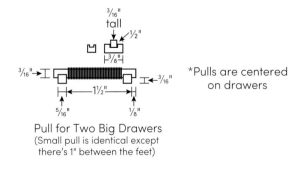

*Pulls are centered on drawers

Pull for Two Big Drawers
(Small pull is identical except there's 1" between the feet)

DRAWING

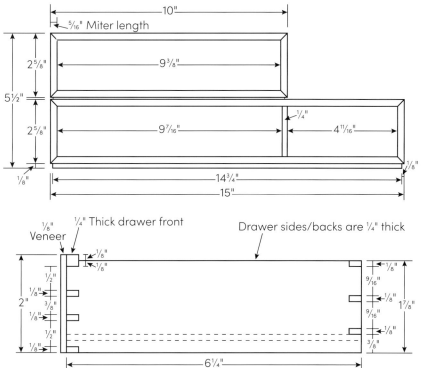

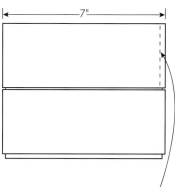

Rabbet for back is ⅛" deep
by ⁵⁄₁₆" wide
Backs are ¼" plywood with
milk paint on outside faces

¹⁄₈" Veneer

¼" Thick drawer front

Drawer sides/backs are ¼" thick

THE GRAIN FLOWS UP AND OVER

You need three boards to make this box. You get the two left ends, the upper box's top and its right end from one. From the second you get the lower box's top and right end. The third board gives you the bottom for both boxes.

---

1   **CUT ENDS FOR THE TWO BOXES.** A spacer (12½ in. long) between the stop (set for the length of the bottom box's top) determines the length. Cut the left side of the bottom box first, then cut the left side of the top box.

2 THE UPPER BOX TOP IS THIRD. Remove the spacer for the box ends, replacing it with a shorter (5 in. long) spacer. Cut the top from the board, and place it in sequence with the two ends you just cut on your bench or saw table. Cut the bottom for the upper box from a separate board at this time.

3 WRAP THE GRAIN DOWN THE OTHER SIDE. The last part cut from this board is the right end of the top box. Put the longest spacer against the stop (remove the other one first) and crosscut it to length. Mark the four parts you cut to indicate their locations in the completed boxes.

4 SWITCH TO A SECOND BOARD. Square up one end, then place the end against the stop. Do not use a spacer. After cutting the top of the lower box, cut its bottom too, but from a separate board.

5 FOLLOW THE GRAIN DOWN THE SECOND END. Put the longest spacer in place and cut the lower box's right end to length. Mark the top and right end to keep them in order.

BUILD THE BOXES

Although these boxes are much wider than the others in this book, blue painter's tape is all you need to secure the joints while the glue dries, if the miters are cut at 45° and square to the edges. Make sure your sled is set up properly, and work deliberately and thoughtfully.

6 **DADOES THE DIVIDER.** Use a ³⁄₁₆-in.-diameter downcut spiral bit in a router table. Cut into the back of the top and stop ³⁄₁₆ in. from the front edge.

7 **DROP THE BOTTOM.** Because you shouldn't rout through the front edge, lower the box's bottom onto the bit carefully. Ideally, it starts cutting ³⁄₁₆ in. from the front edge, but it's OK to start farther away than that. You can lengthen the dado with a chisel afterward.

8 **MITER THE ENDS.** Wide miters can be difficult to cut accurately. Move the sled with a steady hand, pushing in line with the miter bar. Also, make sure that the parts are flat on the sled throughout the cut.

9 **KEEP YOUR FINGERS CLEAR.** The box ends are very short, so use a piece of plywood to press them down. This elevates your hand enough to keep it a safe distance from the spinning blade.

10 **BLUE TAPE WORKS ON BIG JOINTS, TOO.** As with small joints, the key is to press the miters together tightly, so that one side is just a bit under its mate. They will align properly when you roll up the box, but because the tape doesn't stretch much, the pressure it applies is increased.

11 **KEEP GLUE ON THE SURFACE.** Miter joints are weak when the glue is pulled down into the grain, so before you roll up the box, make sure that there is glue sitting on the endgrain of each miter.

12 **WRAP IT UP.** There should be some resistance when you try to close the last joint.

13 **COVER THE LAST JOINT WITH TAPE.** Tape the outer edges first, then pull the tape down in the middle of the joint. Using several long but narrow pieces is easier and more effective than trying to use a single narrow piece that runs the joint's length.

SPACERS FLOAT THE BOXES

These thin strips are purely aesthetic. Beneath the lower box, the spacers acts as feet, lifting the box and creating a sense of lightness. The one between the two boxes creates visual separation, a reminder that they are two, even though they have been joined to make one. And the shadow line they both create gives some depth and dimensionality to the box.

14   **MITERS AT THE CORNER.** Start with a long blank for the front spacer. Stand it on edge and cut the first miter.

15   **TRIM THE FRONT SPACER TO LENGTH.** After marking the length of the spacer (it's ¼ in. shorter than the box's length), cut it to length.

16   **THE FIRST OF TWO GLUES.** Cyanoacrylate glue sets very quickly, which means you don't need to clamp the spacer in place. That means you can work faster and without having clamps in the way.

17 **DROP IN SOME YELLOW GLUE.** PVA woodworking glue creates a strong and long-lasting bond. After putting a bead between the runs of cyanoacrylate, spread it to cover the surface between them.

18 **HOLD THE SPACER IN PLACE.** Use an adjustable square to locate it ⅛ in. from the front edge and both ends then pinch the spacer to the box. Hold it for 20 – 30 seconds. After the cyanoacrylate glue sets, it acts like a clamp, holding the spacer in place while the yellow glue dries.

19 **MARK THE SIDE'S LENGTH.** The first end has been mitered, so press it tightly against miter on the front spacer. Mark the opposite end ⅛ in. from the box's back edge.

20 **THE BACK IS SQUARE.** Use a stop so that you can cut all four side spacers at the same time. Stand the spacer on edge, because it's easier to register the miter's point against the stop in this orientation. Laid down, the miter's point might slip between the stop and sled's fence.

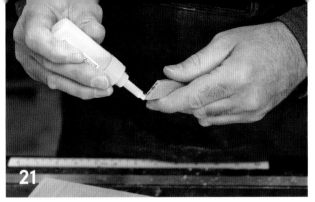

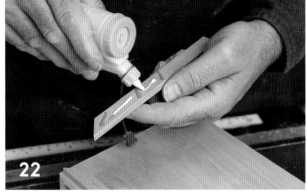

21 **GLUE THE MITER.** A few drops of cyanoacrylate glue keeps the joint closed tightly.

22 **DON'T GLUE THE BACK END.** Alternate between PVA and cyanoacrylate glue and cover only the front half. Because the back half is not glued to the box, the box can expand and contract without breaking the glue joint.

23 **PRESS IT DOWN.** Squeeze as tightly as you can without moving the spacer. Hold it for 20 – 30 seconds.

24 **THE BACK FITS BETWEEN THE SIDES.** The backside of the cabinet will almost never be seen, so there's no aesthetic reason to use a miter joint here. More importantly, the box is going to expand and contract, which it can do freely when the back spacer is tucked between the two side spacers.

25 **ADD THE DIVIDER.** Mill it to fit inside the dadoes then cut the notches. Do not spread glue to the front of the dadoes, because the divider will push it forward as you slide it in. Also, make sure that it doesn't push the top and bottom out. If it does, it's too long.

GLUE THE BOXES TOGETHER

As you did when gluing on the spacers, use glue only on the front half of the sides. Glue the front completely, but use no glue on the back.

26 **ALIGN THE FRONTS.** A tall piece of plywood ensures that the front edges are in the same plane. Check the left end, too.

27 **GIVE THEM THE CLAMPS.** Quick clamps like these can pull parts out of alignment, so keep an eye on that. If they do, remove the clamps, realign, and give it another go.

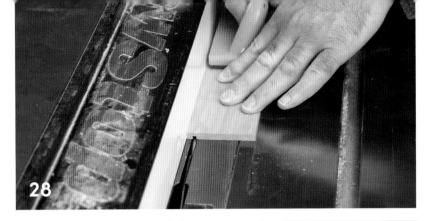

FINGER JOINTS FOR THE DRAWERS

Dovetails would be fine here, but it's good to stretch your joinery legs every now and then. It's also a good idea to explore joinery from a design perspective. Finger joints are quite strong, so suitable for a drawer, and spaced like dovetails, they're aesthetically pleasing, as well.

28 **THE BOTTOM FITS IN A GROOVE.** Use a rip blade with a flat-tooth grind to cut grooves along the bottom edge of all the drawer parts.

29 **CHECK THE FIT.** After gluing decorative paper (I'm using chiyogami, made in Japan) to both sides of a square of ⅛ in. plywood, try to put it into the groove. Most likely it won't fit.

30 **ADD BLUE TAPE TO THE FENCE.** Don't try to move the fence. A piece of tape will adjust the groove a controlled amount. Rip the groove again and test the sample again. Continue to add blue tape until the sample fits in the groove.

31 **DON'T DAMAGE THE PAPER.** The bottom should fit without wiggle, but don't force it like you (foolishly) might with solid wood. Likely, the paper will catch and get damaged. So, make sure the bottom sample slides into the groove without the paper catching on the edges.

32

32 NOTCH THE DRAWER SIDES. These finger joints are cut just as the joints used to join the Box 8 (see pp. 126 – 139). Start by cutting wide, not uniformly sized, fingers on the drawer sides.

33 CUT MATING JOINTS IN THE FRONT AND BACK. After transferring the fingers to the drawer sides, cut the sockets into which the fingers fit. Remember not to cut away the pencil line, because it's entirely on material that should be kept.

33

34 REMOVE THE GROOVE. The bottom slides into the drawer from the back after it has been glued together, which is possible only if the drawer back is cut short.

34

35 GLUE UP THE DRAWER. Clamp the joint from both directions, so that it closes tightly against both shoulders. Remove the clamps, and if they joints stay closed there is no need to put them back on.

36 KEEP IT SQUARE. It's far easier to fit a square drawer, so compare the diagonals to one another. If they match, the drawer is square. If they don't, press the two corners of the longer diagonal toward one another and remeasure.

37 GLUE ON THE VENEER. After the glue has dried for a day and you've cleaned up the front, spread glue, tape the veneer to the drawer, and clamp it beneath a plywood caul. Check around all four edges for spots where the veneer doesn't touch the front. Use additional clamps to close the gaps.

38 ROUT IT FLUSH. Ride the bearing of a flush-trim bit against the drawer front. Start on the endgrain, and work around the drawer.

WRAP THE PULLS IN THREAD

There are easier ways to make pulls, but the color and texture of the thread run around the bar of these pulls is an aesthetic joy. The technique is same one show on pp. 99 – 101.

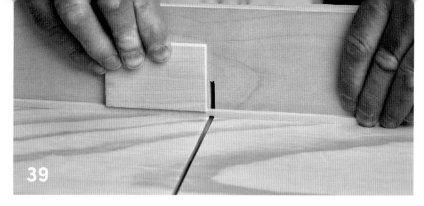

39 START WITH A SINGLE NOTCH. On a blank for all of the feet sized ⁵⁄₁₆" thick, ³⁄₁₆" tall and approximately 15" long. Then cut it with a standard-kerf flat-top-grind rip blade set to cut ¹⁄₁₆ in. into the blank. (see pp. 99 – 101)

40 FINGER JOINT JIG REGULATES SPACING. The registration pin in the jig is ⁵⁄₈ in. from the blade. Put the first notch onto the pin and cut a second notch. Put the second notch on the pin to cut a third, and repeat until you've cut 10 – 12 notches.

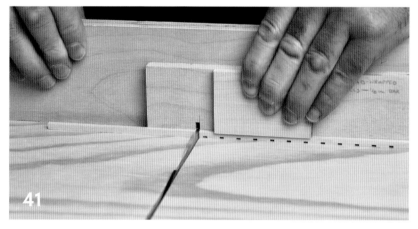

41 USE THE JIG TO CUT THE FEET FREE. Move the jig so that the registration pin is ¹⁄₈ in. from the blade. Put the first notch on the pin and trim its end to length.

42 FLIP THE STICK FOR THE OTHER SIDE. Turn the blank 180° and put the first notch over the pin again. Trim the second end of the foot to length, cutting it free from the blank in the process. Repeat this process for the remaining feet.

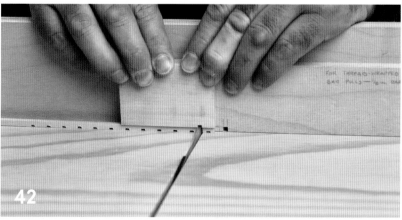

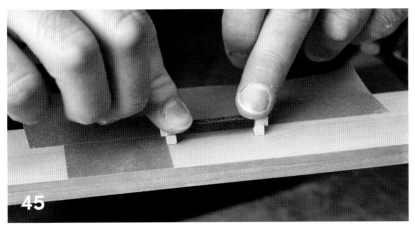

43 GLUE THE FOOT TO THE BAR. Use PVA glue, and inset the foot ⅛ in. from the bar's end. If the bar fits snugly, there is no need to clamp it while the glue dries.

44 LAY DOWN THE THREAD. Wrap over one of the loose ends to secure it under the bar. Continue wrapping toward the other end, then add a second thread, formed into a loop, and wrap over. The loose end of the wrapping thread goes through the loop when you reach the other foot and the loose ends of the loop are pulled, bringing the wrapping thread back under itself.

45 GLUE THE PULL TO THE DRAWER. Blue painter's tape both shows you where the pulls goes and provides positive registration for the feet when you center it on the front.

46 FINISH WITH SHELLAC. Nothing makes figure sing like clear shellac. I used three coats, sanding with P-800 between coats. See pp. 38 – 39 for a more detailed explanation.

Box 10

JEWELRY CABINET ON STAND

There are many pieces of Shaker furniture—benches, step stools, cabinets, and trunks—with sides that extend to floor where a cutout, often a half-circle, is used to create two feet. It's an elegant and beautiful way to create stable footing for furniture. Those Shaker pieces are the inspiration for this small cabinet. I've clearly made a big change: The feet are no longer connected to the case sides, but, and this is important, the feet are cut sequentially from the same board used to make the sides and top of the cabinet. The grain runs up the foot and cabinet side, across the top, and back down the other side to the second foot. So, even though there is space between the base and cabinet, they are tied together. It's a nifty and subtle way to bring two distinct parts together, and shows the power of wood grain. Speaking of grain, vertical grain Douglas fir, especially when it's super tight, is stunning. But it can also be overwhelming, which is why I decided to put a liner inside the case, and paint it and the dividers with green milk paint. The liner and dividers create just enough separation between the case and drawer fronts to restrain the fir so that it's quietly beautiful rather than ostentatious. The liners and dividers also emphasize the cabinet's structure and the shape of the drawer fronts. The cabinet is a wonderful lesson in how structure, grain, color, and part arrangement can be woven together to create stunning furniture.

TOOLS

+ Jointer
+ Planer
+ Bandsaw
+ Tablesaw
+ Miter gauge
+ Dado set
+ Combination blade ground for dovetails
+ Router table
+ Spiral downcut bits (1/8" and 3/16")
+ Rotary cutter

MATERIALS

+ Vertical-grain Douglas fir
+ Basswood
+ Cocobolo
+ Plywood
+ Chiyogami paper
+ Milk paint

PARTS LIST

PART	L	W	T
Base Legs	2"	7"	3/8"
Base Top	15"	7"	3/8"
Cabinet Top/Bottom	15"	7"	3/8"
Cabinet Sides	10 1/2"	7"	3/8"
Outer Spacer	6 3/4"	3/8"	3/8"
Middle Spacer	6 3/4"	1/4"	3/8"
Liner Top/Bottom	14 1/4"	6 9/16"	1/4"
Liner Sides	9 3/4"	6 9/16"	1/4"
Vertical Divider	10"	6 9/16"	1/4"
Right Horizontal Divider	8 3/8"	6 9/16"	1/8"
Left Horizontal Divider	5 1/8"	6 9/16"	1/8"
Right Drawer Front/Back	8 1/2"	3"	1/4"
Right Drawer Sides	6 1/4"	3"	1/4"
Right Drawer Bottom	8 1/4"	6"	1/8"
Right Drawer Pull	1 1/2"	5/16"	3/16"
Left Drawer Front/Back	5"	1 3/4"	1/4"
Left Drawer Sides	6 1/4"	1 3/4"	1/4"
Left Drawer Bottom	4 3/4"	6"	1/8"
Left Drawer Pull	1"	5/16"	3/16"

DRAWING

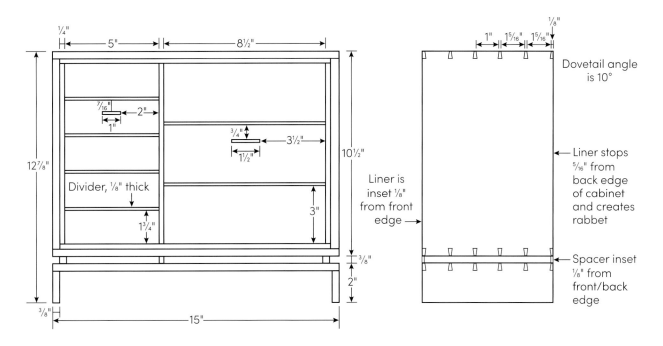

Divider, ⅛" thick

Dovetail angle is 10°

Liner stops 5/16" from back edge of cabinet and creates rabbet

Liner is inset ⅛" from front edge →

Spacer inset ⅛" from front/back edge

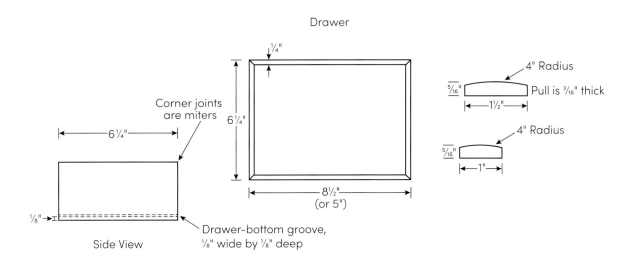

Drawer

Corner joints are miters

Side View

Drawer-bottom groove, ⅛" wide by ⅛" deep

4" Radius
Pull is 3/16" thick

4" Radius

HIDE THE FLATSAWN EDGES

The one negative of quartersawn boards is that their edges have flatsawn grain, which is, to be honest, rather ugly, especially on Douglas fir. So, glue a strip of quartersawn stock over the edge. After the glue is dry, run the edge through the tablesaw so that the veneer is about 1/32 in. thick; this effectively hides the veneer's flatsawn edge and no one, not even you, will know it's there.

1 **COVER THE FRONT EDGE.** Cut a strip of vertical grain Douglas fir that's about 1/8 in. thick and 3/8 in. wide. Although you'll trim the veneer's thickness later, starting out thick makes it easier to glue it to the board.

2 **TAPE THE VENEER IN PLACE.** Use blue painters tape to pull the thin strips tight to the board. There should not be any gaps between the strip and the board.

3 **USE THE BOARDS AS CAULS.** Orient the boards so that the two veneered edges are facing one another then clamp the boards together. Because they are so wide, they will spread the clamping pressure over a wide area, and the pressure from one clamp will overlap the pressure from those next to it. That makes for very tight and clean glue lines.

CUT THE SIDES FOR FLOWING GRAIN

To make the legs, sides, and top of the cabinet you need a single board that's long enough for those parts plus 6 – 8 extra inches. The parts are cut sequentially from the board so that the grain runs up, over, and back down the base and cabinet.

4 **CUT OFF THE SNIPE.** Parts that are uniform in thickness are easier to work with when cutting joinery and cleaning up the joints after the cabinet is assembled.

5 **START WITH A LEG.** Attach a stop block to the sled's fence 15 in. from the blade (the cabinet top's length), then put a spacer block in place to cut the leg. The square end goes against the spacer.

6 **THE CASE SIDE COMES NEXT.** Remove the first spacer, and use a second one (4½ in. long) to cut the cabinet side. Slide the board against the spacer and make the cut.

7   **TAKE THE GRAIN OVER THE TOP.** Remove the spacer, slide the board against the stop and cut the cabinet top to length.

8   **HEAD BACK DOWN THE OTHER SIDE.** Put the spacer for the cabinet side back in place and cut the second one.

9   **THE SECOND LEG IS LAST.** This one is cut using the same spacer used to cut the first one, and there should be no snipe on it.

10 **CUT THE REMAINING PARTS.** To make the cabinet bottom and the top of the base, remove the spacer and use the stop to determine their length. The grain on these parts is irrelevant because it will never be seen.

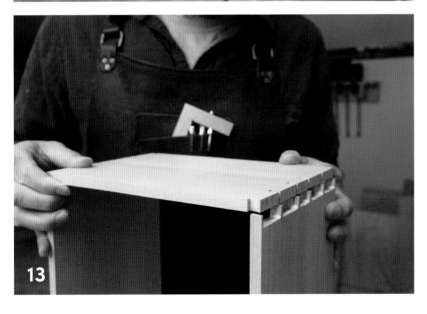

DOVETAILS DELIGHT AT THE CORNERS

Perhaps I'm a bit tightly wound about such things, but I think it's critical that the dovetails on the base and case mirror one another. This is why I cut the tails at the tablesaw with a blade that has all its teeth ground to 10° in the same direction. Using a sled and stop, I can cut tails on all the parts that are perfectly aligned with one another. See pp. 106 –110 for a detailed explanation of the process.

11 **START WITH THE TAILS.** Because I am using a stop to locate the parts for each cut, I lay them out on just one end of one board. Tape the cabinet sides and legs together in matching pairs to cut your work in half.

12 **BOX JOINT BLADES FOR THE PINS.** Unlike a dado set, box joint blades cut a truly flat bottom, which means there is no paring to do on the shoulder.

13 **GLUE THE CASE TOGETHER.** When you clamp the joints, use cauls to spread the pressure and to prevent the clamps from denting the Douglas fir. Don't forget to check that the cabinet is square. If it's not you'll have endless trouble with the liner, dividers, and drawers.

LINER AND DIVIDERS SLIDE INTO THE CASE

Rather than cutting dadoes in the cabinet parts and then housing the dividers in them, make a liner that houses them and fits into the cabinet. The biggest practical advantage to this approach is that there no need to rabbet the cabinet parts for the back, because the liner is cut narrower than the cabinet and creates a rabbet at the back when put into place.

14 **FIT THE LINERS.** The sides fit between the top and bottom to help hold them in place, and butt joints are better than miter joints here, because the straight line where they meet mirrors the straight line between the dovetailed parts of the cabinet and base.

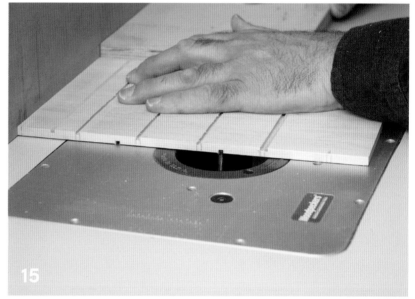

15 **ROUT DADOES FOR THE DIVIDERS.** These are just over 1/16 in. deep, which is deep enough for the light-duty dividers, but not so deep that they weaken the vertical divider. Use a 1/8-in.-diameter spiral downcut bit to cut them.

16 **USE A SPACER WITH THE LINER SIDES.** The vertical divider has a 1/8-in.-long tongue on both ends. The liner sides do not. The router's fence is set for the divider, so drop a 1/8-in.-thick spacer between the fence and liner side when routing the dadoes.

17 GLUE GOES ON THE CASE. Once the front edge of the liner is painted, it's ready to be installed. The liner will curl up if you spread the glue on it. Also, keep the glue about 1/16 in. back from where the front edge of the liner will fall. That prevents squeezeout on the front, which is tricky to clean because the liner's edge is already painted.

18 INSET THE LINER. I place the liner closer the front than its final location and then push it back. Use an adjustable square to locate each piece, ensuring that all four are inset 1/8 in.

19 PRESS IN THE SIDES. Lower the back edge into place and push the front edge down. These can be hard to adjust after they are in, but you can tap them into alignment if you put a wide piece of plywood between them and the hammer.

20 CLAMPS KEEP THEM FLAT. If the middle of the liner bows up, add cauls to bring it tight to the cabinet. If it doesn't, it's fine to clamp along the front and back edges only.

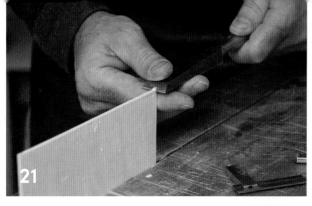

21 **NOTCHES GO PAST THE DADOES.** All of the dividers need to move beyond the end of the stopped dadoes. Notches let them move forward and flush to the liner. After fitting them, tape off the dividers' faces and paint the edges with milk paint.

22 **SLIDE THE DIVIDER IN.** After laying the cabinet face down on your bench, push the divider with both hands to keep it from binding. I put a short bead of glue (about 1 in. long) in the dadoes, starting it ¼ in. from the stopped end.

23 **MAKE IT FLUSH.** I always push the divider past the liner then press it back to get it flush. A small block of plywood is the perfect tool for the job, because it automatically catches on the liner and flushes the divider.

24 **HORIZONTAL DIVIDERS ARE NEXT.** Be gentle with these. At just ⅛ in. thick, they break easily if they bind while you are sliding them in. Use the same block of plywood to get them flush.

ALIGN THE MIDDLE SPACER WITH THE DIVIDER

There are three spacers between the base and the cabinet, and it's probably intuitively compelling to center the middle one between the two on the outside. Don't do that. It will look odd. Instead, make the middle one ¼ in. thick and put it directly below the vertical divider, which is also ¼ in. thick. The other spacers are 5/16 in. thick to match the cabinet sides.

25 **SADDLE SQUARE MAKES IT EASY.** After pressing one leg against the vertical divider, slide the spacer between the cabinets and base and butt it against the square's other leg. Use a pencil to mark its location on the base.

26 **ONLY GLUE THE FRONT END.** With the front secured, the inset will not change as the cabinet expands and contracts, and because the back half isn't glued, the cabinet and base can move without tearing free of the spacers.

27 **JOIN THE CASE AND BASE.** Use some bench horses to elevate the cabinet and plywood cauls to prevent damage to the case. The legs in particular would be easy to break under the extreme pressure that clamps apply.

MITERED DRAWERS ARE PERFECT FOR THE JOB

Dovetails are strong and beautiful, but they are overkill for the drawers in a jewelry cabinet. You're not storing gold doubloons and plumbum in them, after all. So, use miters instead. Their clean, modern look is just right for this cabinet's modern aesthetic, and the joint is plenty strong enough for light duty.

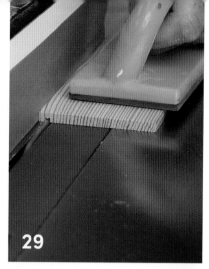

28 **RUN A GROOVE.** The exact depth isn't critical, but it should be less than half the drawer parts' thickness. Also, use a standard-kerf rip blade with a flat top grind.

29 **ADD TAPE AND RUN IT AGAIN.** The drawer bottom, which has paper on both sides, is thicker than the blade's kerf. The simplest way to widen the groove in small increments is by putting a piece of blue painter's tape on the fence, and recutting the groove.

30 **MAKE A SMALL SAMPLE OF THE BOTTOM WITH PAPER ON BOTH FACES.** If the sample doesn't fit in the groove add another piece of tape and cut the groove again. Repeat the process until the bottom slides in without the paper catching.

31 **CUT PARTS TO LENGTH.** The sides are all the same length. The front and back of each drawer should be the same length, too.

32 **THE FRONT LEADS THE WAY.** After fitting it for height, rip the other drawer parts to the same width. Do this for each drawer individually, because there is no guarantee that the pockets are the same height.

33 **MICRO-ADJUST MITERS.** The trick is to cut right to the top edge of the drawer part without cutting it shorter. If you start shy of this and make small adjustments to the micro-adjust jig, you can dial in the cut to perfection.

34 **COVER BOTH SIDES OF THE BOTTOM.** Use spray adhesive (applied to the plywood), press the paper on—take care not to introduce wrinkles and creases—then cut it flush with a rotary cutter. When spraying adhesive for the second side, be sure to put the paper on the other down on a clean surface.

35 **GLUE UP THE DRAWER.** The technique is exactly like the one used to glue up a mitered box, except that you wrap the sides around the bottom as you roll up them up.

PULLS HAVE A GENTLE CURVE

There are two sets of pulls for this cabinet. Five are for the small drawers on the left, and three are for the larger drawers on the right. It's smart to make them with a jig, both for speed and uniformity. I prefer a simple radius jig for my stationary belt sander, because it's incredibly easy to make, fast, and accurate.

36 **JIG TURNS THE ARC.** A screw acts as the pivot, and joins the jig to a base that is clamped to the sander's table. I do not use a clamp or hold down, because the pull blank fits very tightly into the jig. Rotate the pull slowly into the sander, and there is no need to rough out the shape first.

37 **OFFSET THE PULL.** Admittedly, this is a personal aesthetic choice, but I like the pulls on taller drawers to be above the front's centerline. When locating the pull on the five shorter drawers, offset it less, so that it's proportional to their size.

38 **ADD SOME STOPS.** The wider drawers need two, but the smaller ones require one. After aligning the drawer front flush with the dividers, gently butt the stop against the drawer back and hold it there while cyanoacrylate glue sets, about 20 – 30 seconds.

39 **THE FINISH?** Shellac, of course. Although I do not put shellac on the green milk paint, you can if it makes it easier to finish the cabinet's front edge. Check out pp. 38 – 39 for a complete explanation of how to apply the shellac.

40 **CLAMPS AND CAULS FOR THE BACK.** The back is inset 1/16 in., so the cauls not only spread the clamping pressure, but also make it easier to tighten the clamps into position. Cauls on the front prevent denting.

CONVERSIONS

Fractions to Decimal Equivalents (Inches)				Inches to Millimeters (Fractions to Decimal Equivalents)			
1/64	.015625	33/64	.515625	1/64	0.396875	33/64	13.09688
1/32	.031250	17/32	.531250	1/32	0.793750	17/32	13.49375
3/64	.046875	35/64	.546875	3/64	1.190625	35/64	13.89063
1/16	.062500	9/16	.562500	1/16	1.587500	9/16	14.28750
5/64	.078125	37/64	.578125	5/64	1.984375	37/64	14.68438
3/32	.093750	19/32	.593750	3/32	2.381250	19/32	15.08125
7/64	.109375	39/64	.609375	7/64	2.778125	39/64	15.47813
1/8	.125000	5/8	.625000	1/8	3.175000	5/8	15.87500
9/64	.140625	41/64	.640625	9/64	3.571875	41/64	16.27188
5/32	.156250	21/32	.656250	5/32	3.968750	21/32	16.66875
11/64	.171875	43/64	.671875	11/64	4.365625	43/64	17.06563
3/16	.187500	11/16	.687500	3/16	4.762500	11/16	17.46250
13/64	.203125	45/64	.703125	13/64	5.159375	45/64	17.85938
7/32	.218750	23/32	.718750	7/32	5.556250	23/32	18.25625
15/64	.234375	47/64	.734375	15/64	5.953125	47/64	18.65313
1/4	.250000	3/4	.750000	1/4	6.350000	3/4	19.05000
17/64	.265625	49/64	.765625	17/64	6.746875	49/64	19.44688
9/32	.281250	25/32	.781250	9/32	7.143750	25/32	19.84375
19/64	.296875	51/64	.796875	19/64	7.540625	51/64	20.24063
5/16	.312500	13/16	.812500	5/16	7.937500	13/16	20.63750
21/64	.328125	53/64	.828125	21/64	8.334375	53/64	21.03438
11/32	.343750	27/32	.843750	11/32	8.731250	27/32	21.43125
23/64	.359375	55/64	.859375	23/64	9.128125	55/64	21.82813
3/8	.375000	7/8	.875000	3/8	9.525000	7/8	22.22500
25/64	.390625	57/64	.890625	25/64	9.921875	57/64	22.62188
13/32	.406250	29/32	.906250	13/32	10.31875	29/32	23.01875
27/64	.421875	59/64	.921875	27/64	10.71563	59/64	23.41563
7/16	.437500	15/16	.937500	7/16	11.11250	15/16	23.81250
29/64	.453125	61/64	.953125	29/64	11.50938	61/64	24.20938
15/32	.468750	31/32	.968750	15/32	11.90625	31/32	24.60625
31/64	.484375	63/64	.984375	31/64	12.30313	63/64	25.00313
1/2	.500000	1	1.00000	1/2	12.70000	1	25.40000

ABOUT THE AUTHOR

Matt Kenney is a professional box and furniture maker living in Northwest Connecticut. He's written numerous articles about the craft and teaches it throughout the United States and overseas. His first book, *52 Boxes in 52 Weeks* (Taunton Press), chronicles the year he spent making boxes in order to improve his design skills. While making those boxes, he began to experiment with kumiko, and his love for its geometric beauty and elegance led to his second book, *The Art of Kumiko* (Blue Hills Press). You can keep an eye on what he's up to in the shop by following him on Instagram (@mekwoodworks). In addition to making furniture, writing, and teaching, Matt is father to two teenagers, hikes the woods and mountains of New England, and stands in rivers trying to catch trout with a fly rod.

ALSO BY MATT KENNEY

For more from Matt Kenney, find *The Art of Kumiko* at bluehillspress.com.

Text © 2021 by Blue Hills Press
Photography @ Joe Faraoni, except where noted.
Photography @ Matt Kenney: cover and pages 2, 3, 4, 5, 6, 7, 18, 19, 24, 25, 26, 27 38, 39, 40, 41, 52, 53, 54, 55, 68, 69, 70, 71, 86, 87, 102, 103, 124, 125, 126, 127, 140, 141, 156, 157

Publisher & Editor: Matthew Teague
Design: Lindsay Hess
Layout: Alicia Freile
Photography: Joe Faraoni & Matt Kenney
Copy Editor: Megan Fitzpatrick
Index: Jay Kreider

Blue Hills Press
P.O. Box 239
Whites Creek, TN 37189

Paperback: 978-1-951217-26-6
Hardback: 978-1-951217-44-0
eBook ISBN: 978-1-951217-34-1
Library of Congress Control Number: 2021945367
Printed in China
10 9 8 7 6 5 4 3 2

Note: The following list contains names used in *Build Better Boxes* that may be registered with the United State Copyright Office: Old Fashioned Milk Paint Co.; Scotch; Frog Tape; Babe Bot; Renaissance Wax; Taklone; *Fine Woodworking*

INDEX

Note: Page numbers in *italics* indicate projects.

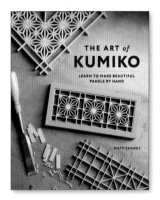
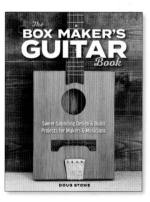
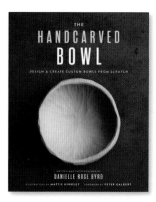
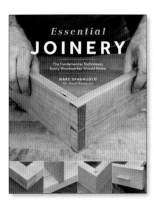

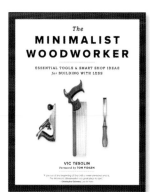